COMMiTMENT

COMMITMENT

OLAV MAASSEN
CHRIS MATTS
CHRIS GEARY

Hathaway te Brake Publications
Amsterdam - London

ISBN: 978-94-6241-003-9

First published in the Netherlands in 2013
by Hathaway te Brake Publications

First print May 2013
Second print January 2016

Version 1.0.1 (Berlin release)

Cover design: Chris Geary with Olav Maassen and Chris Matts

CHAPTER ONE

13

THE INDIGO RELEASE HAS A RAG STATUS OF AMBER WITH THE RISING PERCEPTION THAT IT HAS A HIGHER PROBABILITY OF BREACHING THE RED COVENANTS.

STATUS IS AMBER.

WE WILL KNOW FOR CERTAIN WHETHER WE CAN HIT THE DEADLINE BY THURSDAY WHEN THE CLIENT COMES IN TO CHECK IT OUT AGAIN.

clkk clkk clkk clkk clkk clkk clkk clkk clkk clkk clkk clkk clkk

DO YOU WANNA JOIN US FOR A DRINK TO START OFF THE WEEKEND?

NO THANKS. I HAVE SOME WORK TO FINISH UP.

FAIR ENOUGH. MAYBE NEXT WEEK.

MAYBE. HAVE A GOOD NIGHT, SEE YOU MONDAY.

WHY DID YOU ASK HER?

NOTHING WRONG WITH BEING FRIENDLY.

YEAH, RIGHT...

clkk clkk clkk clkk clkk clkk clkk clkk clkk

17

NIGHT. SEE YOU MONDAY.

NIGHT. HAVE A GOOD WEEKEND.

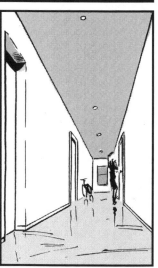

YOUR MOTHER WOULD BE LIVID SEEING YOU WALK AROUND WITH WET HAIR LIKE THAT, YOUNG LADY.

WHAT ARE YOU DOING HERE?

SO WHERE IS IT?

THE FUNKY FUNGUS

WHERE'S WHAT?

MY BIRTHDAY PRESENT.

YOU MEAN THE MEAL YOU JUST ATE?

WHAT? THAT'S NOT FAIR. IF I HAD KNOWN I WOULD HAVE ORDERED THE STEAK.

AH WELL, BETTER LUCK NEXT TIME.

SO COME ON THEN WHAT DID YOU DO FOR YOUR BIRTHDAY?

NOTHING. DAVID NEEDED SOMETHING DONE FOR TOMORROW.

YOU WORKED?! YOU WORKED LATE ON YOUR BIRTHDAY?!

YOU'RE TELLING ME YOU WORKED LATE ON YOUR THIRTIETH BIRTHDAY?!

IT WAS EITHER THAT OR GO IN AT FIVE TOMORROW.

THAT MIGHT BE SLIGHTLY FORGIVABLE. WHAT DID YOU DO LAST NIGHT?

STAYED IN.

ALONE? SO THE ONLY THING YOU DID ON YOUR BIRTHDAY WAS WORK WITH DAVID?

DAVID WASN'T THERE. HE WENT HOME EARLY.

CAN'T BELIEVE THIS. WE'VE SPOKEN ABOUT THIS BEFORE.

IF YOU'RE LIKE THIS AT THIRTY, WHAT ARE YOU GONNA BE LIKE AT SIXTY?

I'M NOT LETTING YOU GET AWAY WITH THIS.

YEAH, WELL...

IF YOU KEEP FOLLOWING DAVID AROUND LIKE THAT, YOU'LL TURN INTO A MOANY OLD MAID SOON.

OH THANKS. I'M NOT TH --

'SCUSE ME, LADIES. THESE ARE FROM THE TWO GENTLEMEN OVER THERE.

WHAT? I DON --

SHUDDUP. ARE THEY CUTE?

DON'T LOOK. YOU'LL ONLY ENCOURAGE THEM.

SO WHAT? THEY DON'T LOOK TOO BAD.

AND NOT TOO DRUNK, WE COULD BE ONTO SOMETHING HERE.

YOU CALL THEM OVER AND I'M GOING HOME.

25

AH, LILLY AND ROSE...

...WHAT A BEAUTIFUL BOUQUET YOU MAKE.

IS THAT IT? THAT'S HOW YOU'RE GOING TO SWEEP US OFF OUR FEET?

STILL, I THINK WE'RE LUCKY YOU DIDN'T CALL US A 'PAIR OF RARE BLOOMS'.

I-- I.. ER, I DI --

LOOK, SORRY TO SOUND A BIT RUDE, BUT MY SISTER AND I HAVEN'T SEEN EACH OTHER IN A WHILE.

WE'RE BOUND TO BE BACK AT SOME POINT, HOW ABOUT WE TALK SOME MORE THEN?

WE'LL KEEP THE DRINKS, THANK YOU VERY MUCH.

WHY DON'T WE GET ANOTHER ROUND IN, AND SEE IF WE CAN'T CHANGE YOUR MINDS?

WHAT DO YOU THINK ROSE?

WELL THAT ABOUT SAYS IT ALL, DOESN'T IT?

BETTER LUCK NEXT TIME.

CAN I FACEBOOK YOU?

OH, AND YOU WERE SO CLOSE...

27

SORRY ABOUT THAT. JUST WASN'T IN THE MOOD.

S'ALRIGHT. YOUR BIRTHDAY, CAN DO WHAT YOU WANT.

THANKS.

OF COURSE THAT DOES MEAN WE'RE GOING TO DO WHATEVER I WANT TO DO ON MY BIRTHDAY.

I SUPPOSE I ASKED FOR THAT.

JUST TRY NOT TO MAKE IT TOO PAINFUL.

WHAT'RE YOU DOING?

HANG ON. IT'S IN HERE SOMEWHERE.

I WAS JUST ABOUT TO GIVE YOU SOMETHING BEFORE THEY CAME OVER.

A TATTY BIT OF PAPER?

IT WILL CHANGE YOUR LIFE.

IT'S A BUSINESS CARD.

DOES IT COME WITH SOME MAGIC BEANS?

I'M SERIOUS, ROSE. CALL THOSE PEOPLE.

YOU WON'T REGRET IT.

29

Dear Susan,

Just got back from the West End with Lil. She wanted to do something for my 30th birthday. How could I refuse spending some time with my sister? We even encountered two guys who were hitting on us and I'm sure Lil would have had us waste the whole evening with them. You could tell they were not interested in anything other than a one night stand. Luckily they got my hints after a few minutes.

Lil gave me grief about David again. What she forgets, is that David was the ONLY person who would hire me after Nimrod bombed. David may get me to do a lot but he has been a good and loyal friend. Not only did he give me a job after Nimrod, he has given me every job since. Not everyone can join a dot com, some of us actually have to have a bit of stability in their lives.

Lil went on about that "Ski Trip" story again. It's like she hasn't told me about it a hundred times already. You know what, I'll just write it down now so that I can remember the details and interrupt her with them next time. That way, she might give me a break.
So Susan, I present Lilly Randall's Most Marvellous Ski Trip.

Lilly had booked a ski trip with friends for a weekend, but later realized she had to be in the London office early in the morning the next Monday for a business presentation. Her flight was scheduled to return to Stansted Airport at 11pm, which was pretty late at night. She checked the time of the last train to London from Stansted to find out it was at 11.30pm. That was okay as long as her flight landed on time, got through customs quickly and there was no delay with her luggage. Then she would make it to the train for London in time. Given the flight was from an airport near to a ski resort, it was possible the flight might be delayed... by snow or all manner of things.

She didn't want to cancel the ski trip and miss out on the fun and she had to be in the office on Monday, so she decided to look for options. Something she picked up in a "Real Options" course.

She started looking at hotels near Stansted. Found a couple but she would have to pay for the hotel unless she was able to cancel by 6pm. No good as this meant she was committed to a night in the hotel. Instead, she made a list of hotels at the airport so she could ring them to see if they had anything free when she needed them.

She considered taxis. Black cabs are expensive and if the flight landed late she would be fighting with the rest of the flight for those available. If her bag was off first, that was fine, but if it wasn't, she was at the back of the queue. She considered a minicab from her local firm which would be cheaper and more reliable as she used them ALL the while. She makes a big deal out of building a relationship with them. The problem is that the journey is an hour and she would not know if she needed it until after they had to set off. She wrote down a list of mini-cabs close to the airport so that she could call them as soon as she knew she had missed the train.

She had her options to get home from the airport: get the train, mini-cab close to the airport, black cab, hotel at the airport.

She called the mini-cab companies to find out which ones might have a cab on a Sunday night. She called the hotels at the airport to see which ones had free rooms.

For some reason, she stopped and asked herself "What is my goal?" All the while she had been focused on getting home on Sunday night. She asked herself "Why?" (Susan, I sometimes think "Why" from Annie Lennox's Diva album should be the theme tune to Lil's Ski Trip Story). Why do I want to get home on Sunday night?

I love the theatrical way she delivers the next bit. "AND I REALISED THAT GETTING HOME WAS NOT MY GOAL!" Hushed tones "My goal was to be at work on Monday morning before 9am. And I need to be showered, nice smelling and as fresh as a carnation." She realised that she did not care where she stayed the night as long as she could get to work on time. So she left a freshly pressed suit and blouse and clean shoes in the coat cupboard in her office. That was all she really needed to ensure she could stay anywhere on Sunday night.

In the end a friend on the trip had a change of plans and offered to give her a lift home. As they drove home at 1am she realised her friend would have an additional hour driving in order to give a lift home. She ended up crashing in her friend's spare room. She showered at her friend's place, travelled into work with them and got dressed into her work clothes in the toilet at the office.

And she has never shut up about the story since. And that is why she now keeps a clean suit in my apartment. Just in case.   Night Susan.

CHAPTER TWO

OH, HEY, HOW'D IT GO?

WHAT'S GOING ON, DAVID?

WHY ARE YOU PACKING YOUR STUFF?

EXCUSE ME -- ROSE? COULD YOU STEP THIS WAY PLEASE?

EXCUSE ME?

IT IS ROSE, ISN'T IT?

...YES...

GREAT. IF YOU'D LIKE TO COME INSIDE.

PLEASE COME IN, ROSE.

SORRY TO SURPRISE YOU LIKE THAT --

-- THIS WON'T TAKE LONG.

ROSE, AN EXCITING OPPORTUNITY HAS ARISEN FOR YOU.

DAVID WASN'T DELIVERING. THE PROJECT NEEDS SOMEONE WHO CAN DELIVER.

WE HAVE LOOKED AT YOUR BACKGROUND AND EXPERIENCE AND WE THINK YOU WOULD BE PERFECT FOR WHAT WE NEED.

WE HAVE HAD TO LET DAVID GO AND WE WANT YOU TO TAKE ON HIS RESPONSIBILITIES.

I NORMALLY WORK FOR DAVID. I'M NOT SURE IF I'M THE RIGHT PERSON FOR THIS.

I'M CERTAIN OTHERS ARE BETTER QUALIFIED.

35

WELL, HELLO. HOW'S YOUR DAY BEEN?

PRETTY AWFUL... I'M NOT DISTURBING YOU, AM I?

NO. JUST GETTING READY FOR ANOTHER EXHAUSTING NIGHT ON THE TOWN.

BUT LET ME GUESS, YOU'RE STILL AT WORK...

YEAH, BU--

OOOHHH, WE TALKED ABOUT THIS. PUT DAVID ON THE PHONE.

CAN'T. HE'S GONE. BEEN FIRED.

WHAT?! SO WHAT DOES THAT MEAN ABOUT YOU?

THEY GAVE ME HIS JOB.

YAYYY. ABOUT TIME.

NOW DO WHAT ANY HALF DECENT BOSS WOULD DO AND GO HOME.

TIME TO START DUMPING YOUR WORK ONTO SOME POOR LACKEY.

MAYBE. NOT YET.

YOU DON'T SOUND TOO HAPPY ABOUT THIS.

I DON'T WANT TO BE RESPONSIBLE FOR THE WHOLE DEPARTMENT.

I'VE GOT UNTIL MONDAY TO COME UP WITH A NEW PLAN.

OR YOU GET TO FOLLOW DAVID OUT THE DOOR...

ALONG WITH EVERYONE ELSE!

I WAS HOPING TO AVOID THIS TYPE OF RESPONSIBILITY.

OH, GET OVER YOURSELF. THAT WAS LONG AGO. IT DOESN'T MATTER ANYMORE.

IF YOU REALLY DIDN'T WANT TO DO IT, YOU COULD'VE LEFT WITH DAVID.

SOMETIMES YOU JUST NEED A LITTLE PUSH.

EVEN IF IT'S OFF A CLIFF?

MAYBE. BUT AT LEAST YOU KNOW YOU'LL HIT THE GROUND AT SOME POINT.

NOW THAT'S A CHEERY THOUGHT.

HERE TO HELP.

I NEED TO GO NOW, WE'LL TALK MORE ON WEDNESDAY, OKAY?

YEAH...

DON'T WORRY ABOUT IT. THIS CAN ONLY BE A GOOD THING.

SEEYA.

OKAY...

SO YOU GUYS PROBABLY REALISED THAT DAVID HAS GONE, AND THAT I'VE GOT TO PICK UP HIS ROLE.

SO WHAT DOES THAT MEAN?

WE ARE ALL GOING TO HAVE TO WORK HARDER TO MAKE THE PROJECT A SUCCESS.

I'M COUNTING ON ALL OF YOU.

I'M NOT SURE I LIKE THE SOUND OF WORKING HARDER.

WE ARE ALREADY WORKING AT 110%

LET ME WORK THROUGH THE PLAN SO I CAN TELL YOU WHAT IT MEANS.

RESOURCE	SAM_	UTILISED
RESOUR_		400%
RESOURCE 2	SOURCE	87%
RESOURCE 3	SOURCE	91%
RESOURCE 4	SOURCE	98%
RESOURCE 5	SOURCE	

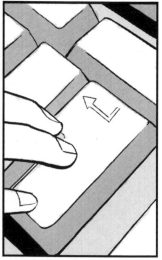

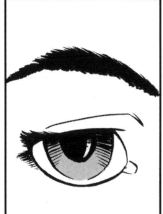

525%

87%

91%

43

SO, I'M SCREWED.

THERE'S NO WAY I CAN DELIVER THE PROJECT.

SO I, AND THE REST OF THE GROUP GET FIRED, AND SOME IDIOT ON ANOTHER FLOOR GETS TO SAVE THE DAY.

OKAY, LET ME EXPLAIN 'REAL OPTIONS' TO YOU.

REMEMBER THE BUSINESS CARD?

WHAT ABOUT IT?

OPTIONS HAVE VALUE, OPTIONS EXPIRE.

NEVER COMMIT EARLY UNLESS YOU KNOW WHY.

WHAT DOES THAT ALL MEAN?

AN OPTION IS SOMETHING WE CAN CHOOSE TO DO.

THEATRE TICKET, AIRLINE TICKET, ETC. IT IS WHERE YOU HAVE THE RIGHT TO DO SOMETHING, BUT NOT AN OBLIGATION.

THE BIGGEST PROBLEM IS THAT MOST PEOPLE SEE COMMITMENTS WHICH ARE ACTUALLY OPTIONS.

A COMMITMENT IS SOMETHING WE HAVE TO DO. TAXES, ETC.

IT'S A PROBLEM WITH THEIR FILTERS OF PERCEPTION.

THAT'S ALL WELL AND GOOD, BUT I NEED SOMETHING I CAN USE RIGHT NOW WHEN I GET BACK TO THE OFFICE

OKAY. TRY THIS...

SO, DO YOU THINK YOU'RE GOING TO BE OKAY FOR THIS AFTERNOON?

I THINK SO. DOESN'T SOUND TOO TRICKY.

I'LL JUS--

OH, HIYA. NEVER SEEN YOU OUT OF THE OFFICE.

WHU--?

ROSE ISN'T IT? FROM THE SECOND FLOOR.

DUNCAN,. FROM THE FOURTH. WE'VE SHARED A FEW MEETINGS HERE AND THERE.

OH, HI...

ALMOST DIDN'T RECOGNISE YOU WITH YOUR HAIR DOWN. VERY NICE.

SORRY ABOUT THAT.

ANYWAY I SEE YOU'RE BUSY.

SEE YOU AROUND SOMETIME.

WHO'S THAT?

JUST SOME IDIOT FROM ANOTHER FLOOR.

WELL IF IT ALL GOES BADLY, YOU COULD ASK IF HE NEEDS AN ASSISTANT.

47

48

EVEN LATER
THAT NIGHT...

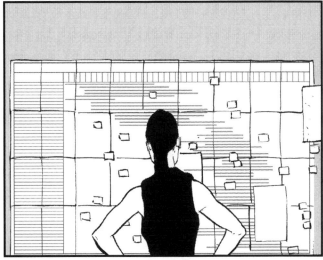

49

Dear Susan,

I had a really great lunch with Lilly yesterday. She was telling me about real options again. I've ignored her in the past but currently I feel in the need of some options... pun intended.

Lilly said that the most important thing is to understand the difference between options and commitments, and when an option is not an option. She said that climbing down a rock face was a commitment. However we can turn that commitment into an option by taking a rope with us. She said that the option needs to be properly tested. Climbing down a rock face with a rope that's not secured was the same as climbing down without one. In order for the commitment to be reversible you need to tie the rope to something at the top and then you can climb back up again. In effect, although the rope provides an option, it is not an option if we start to climb down without the rope tied to the top.

We discussed all sorts of things that were really options rather than commitments. For example tickets (plane, concert and sporting events). Commitments were things like tax, children and dying... no offence. Funnily enough plane tickets are a commitment on the part of the airline. They are committed to transporting you, you have the option to go.

I explained how I was working out the critical path of our project. Effectively the duration of those dependent tasks that specify the earliest date we can finish the project. Lilly seemed bored.

I finally get "Technical Debt". The guys at work go on and on about it as if it's this all-important thing. Anyway my head was spinning from all the talk about "Options", "Expiry Conditions", and "Commitments", and Lilly was talking about "technical debt". I did not hear all she said but she said it's really motivating for a team to feel they are doing quality work. So that's it. The purpose of technical debt is to motivate the team. Important in many cases but perhaps not in our case when we have really important deadlines.

Good night Susan. I'm tired so going to keep it short.

SATURDAY...

I THOUGHT THAT EVERYONE HAD TO COME IN TODAY?

WHERE'S JIM?

THAT'S NOT FAIR! I DON'T HAVE ANY KIDS.

HE REFEREES FOR A SOCCER TEAM ON SATURDAYS.

I'M GONNA --

SSHHH!

-- NOT AS MUCH AS I'M ON NOW, BUT THEY HAVE A MUCH MORE ENLIGHTENED APPROACH TO WORK/LIFE BALANCE.

OH, GOT TO GO.

HIYA, SIMON. WHERE'S BOB?

OH, HE'S SICK TODAY.

TYPICAL. JUST WHAT I NEED.

WE FALL BEHIND NO MATTER WHAT I DO.

51

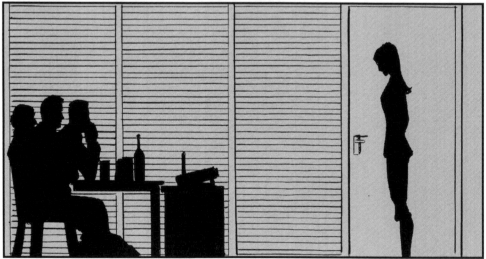

Blobs

RANDOM MUSINGS - LILLY RANDALL

Types of Options

Earliest use of options

Options are not new and Mother Nature is one of the biggest users. The earliest documented usage of real options is the fossils from the Cambrian Era. During the Cambrian Era there was a huge amount of biodiversity. Gradually many of these diverse organisms died out. The diversity was so huge that it is known as the Cambrian Explosion. Quite literally, the conditions on Earth resulted in life creating lots and lots of options.

In our world there are roughly three kinds of options:

- Financial options
- Embedded options
- Real options

Financial Options

When people think of options, they normally think of financial options. Financial Options famously contributed to the "Tulip" bubble in Amsterdam many centuries ago. In the 17th century tulips were very popular in the Netherlands and the demand rose so high that traders wanted to secure the tulips in order for them to be able to sell them. So they bought the right to buy tulips at a later date for a specified amount. This led to a perceived higher demand and a highly speculative market that ultimately crashed.

Financial options have been around for many years but they only really came to the fore when Fischer Black, Myron Scholes and Robert Merton published their famous formula for determining the value of an option in 1973. Since then, the markets for options have grown and grown. The invention of the Black-Scholes equation spawned an entire industry. The key thing about a financial option is that the two parties entering into the option (the buyer of the option, and the seller of the option who takes on a commitment) do so in the understanding that they are entering into an option. The buyer willingly pays a premium for the option, and the maturity / expiry of the option is specified in the options contract.

Embedded Options

A second class of option is the embedded option. An embedded option is an option that occurs in a legal contract, which was NOT specifically intended to be an option. This is a clause in a contract that allows the buyer some flexibility as a kind of service. The seller and the buyer are often unaware that this structure is an embedded option. The seller does not know they have given away an option for free just because it does not look like an option.
The option can be very valuable and the maturity of the option may or may not be specified. It is quite likely the option buyer does NOT pay a premium for the option.

Examples of embedded options include:
• Operational Tolerance in Oil Contracts. Contracts for physical delivery of oil contain an operational tolerance which is a fancy way of saying that both parties do not know which oil tanker (which vary in size) will be used to pick up the oil. To accommodate this variance oil contracts allow for a variable amount to be picked up, for example the contract would be for 100,000 barrels plus or minus 5%.
If you read this same contract from an options perspective, the plus or minus 5% means the contract is really for 95,000 barrels plus an option to buy a further 10,000 barrels.

If the price of oil has gone up above the price in the contract by the time the tanker picks the oil up, the buyer can buy the extra 10,000 barrels cheaper than the current market price. And if the price has gone below the contract price, the tanker takes only the minimum 95,000 barrels.

• Phased contracts. Contracts that contain a specified price for which subsequent goods and services can be bought for are called phased contracts. For example, an IT contract with a specified phase 2 allowing the buyer to buy the second phase at a set price. The buyer can see how much phase 1 costs and potentially change suppliers for phase 2 if he thinks he can get it cheaper. Alternatively if the cost is more than he thought, the buyer can use the offered price for the second phase.

The Black-Scholes equation or one of its many children can be applied to the valuation of an embedded option, but may not always be appropriate. This can happen when the underlying assumptions of the Black-Scholes formula are not all valid, for instance when there is not a single correct price of an underlying asset of the option.

When an expert trader of options identifies an option embedded in a contract, he will price the option separate from the rest of the contract. Understanding this difference between the "market price" and the "market price adjusted for optionality" can be used to create a (market) risk free profit known as an arbitrage. The trick is spotting these options as they are rarely called options.

Real Options

Real options are options that exist outside of legal frameworks. They are the choices we have in the real world. Black-Scholes and its derivative cannot be used to value real options. However, some of the things we know from financial mathematics mean that we can say three things about real options....

Recent Posts

September (5)

August (3)

July (4)

June (5)

May (5)

April (4)

March (5)

February (3)

January (6)

Previous Year - (63)

Options have value

Not just the value of the benefit received (intrinsic value), but also the fact that you still have an option has value above the intrinsic value. Being able to choose later is valuable. This value is higher when there is more uncertainty.

Options expire

At some point the option is no longer available. It expires either based on time passing or that other events have happened making it no longer possible to use a particular option. The most important thing to keep track of with real options is the expiry condition(s). Under what condition is an option no longer available.

Never commit early unless you know why

Committing to an option is when you decide to do something and it is no longer optional, but an obligation / commitment. Making a commitment destroys options to realize some value / benefit. With real options it is important to understand why you destroy one thing to create another. It is not about committing as late as possible as that might expose one to higher and unnecessary risks. It is about gathering as much information in the time available and trying to push to expiry conditions to a later date or knowing why you commit earlier than the expiry.

Real options are literally everywhere. Anything you can do without the obligation to do it is a real option: phoning a friend, buying a house, finding a new job, walking up to a stranger, travelling to Cuba.

As soon as you understand this, you'll see them everywhere. No worries, relax. You don't have to manage them all, just the ones that are most important to you.

Seeya next time - L

Recent Posts

September (5)

August (3)

July (4)

June (5)

May (5)

April (4)

March (5)

February (3)

January (6)

Previous Year - (63)

CHAPTER THREE

'MY FAULT'? WHAT ARE YOU TALKING ABOUT?

I DID WHAT YOU TOLD ME TO DO --

-- AND IT'S ALL GONE TO HELL!!!

TELL ME WHAT YOU DID...

YOU RECKON THESE PEOPLE CAN HELP ME...?

IF THEY CAN'T, I CAN CALL OTHERS, BUT THEY DON'T LIVE IN LONDON AND MIGHT TAKE LONGER TO RESPOND.

I'M SORRY I SHOUTED. JUST NEEDED TO LET IT ALL OUT.

NO PROBLEM. YOU SET IT UP, AND I'LL GO ALONG WITH YOU.

THANKS. I'LL CALL YOU WHEN IT'S DONE.

RIGHT, I'VE GOT TO LEAVE EARLY FOR AN IMPORTANT MEETING.

I'LL SEE YOU GUYS IN THE MORNING.

WOW. LEAVING WHILE THE SUN IS STILL SHINING.

SOMETHING WRONG?

NO, NO. GOT A MEETING TO GET TO. DON'T WANT TO BE LATE.

NOT A HOT DATE, I HOPE. DON'T WANT TO BE JEALOUS.

I WISH. JUST WORK RELATED, I'M AFRAID.

WELL THAT'S OKAY THEN.

HOPE IT GOES WELL, SEE YOU IN THE MORNING.

WILL DO. HAVE A GOOD NIGHT.

Blobs

RANDOM MUSINGS - LILLY RANDALL

Recent Posts

October (1)

September (5)

August (3)

July (4)

June (5)

May (5)

April (4)

March (5)

February (3)

January (6)

Previous Year -
(63)

About relationships and knowledge options

Just a quick post before meeting the Cantina guys with Rose. It reminded me that relationships are some of the most valuable options. The ability to ring someone and have them reach out and help you is very special. This is especially true when learning new things. People have different learning styles;
I have trouble learning things straight from a book or blog post. Having someone you can ask questions to when you're at the point you don't understand something speeds up your learning process several-fold. At least it did for me.

Knowledge Options

This ability to learn things quickly lead me to something I call knowledge options. Knowledge options are those pieces of
information I know just enough of. What I do differently
compared to others is that I learn enough about a subject to understand what can be done with the tools, and how long it will take me to learn the tools to the point that I can apply them.

Some subjects take a long while to become competent in so I start to apply them before I need them so that I'm competent with them in case I ever need them. Other subjects I leave until later. In both cases it is useful to know someone who can help me learn.

Another way of creating these knowledge options is to go through the contents pages of books and look for terms and subjects you do not know. A more general approach is to constantly look out for subjects you do not know about.

Finding a mentor

Finding the right mentor for a subject that is available as well can be a challenge. My experience is that practitioners, the people who do this stuff in their daily work, are the best mentors. The practitioners normally can tell you which are the important bits. They have gone through all the material, tried it out, and tossed out the things that didn't work for them. Finding these practitioners is a lot easier nowadays than before.

To find a mentor for a subject, I start with searching for the authors who have published a good book on the subject. I then look for the community of practitioners who gather around the author. Besides the fact that the practitioners have lived through the experience, they normally have more time to spend explaining things to you than a busy author. These days most subjects have a community who meet in an on-line forum (e-mail / Facebook / LinkedIn groups) to discuss the material. The groups are normally very supportive of people asking questions about the subject and provide a very valuable resource.

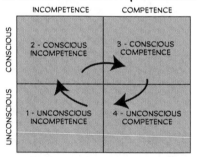

Conscious Incompetence

Knowledge options explicitly acknowledge the value of being consciously incompetent about a subject with one extra criteria: how long it takes to become consciously competent in the subject. If a subject takes a long time to learn and it is likely to be useful, then learn the subject early. If it takes a short time, the learning commitment can be deferred.

The conscious competence model was invented by Noel Burch in 1970, though some incorrectly attribute it to Abraham Maslow.

Recent Posts

October (1)

September (5)

August (3)

July (4)

June (5)

May (5)

April (4)

March (5)

February (3)

January (6)

Previous Year - (63)

RIGHT. SO THERE ARE THREE THINGS YOU NEED TO KNOW ON YOUR PROJECT.

OKAY.

WHERE YOU ARE GOING --

-- WHERE YOU ARE --

-- AND HOW TO GET BETWEEN THE TWO AS QUICKLY AS POSSIBLE.

SOUNDS SIMPLE ENOUGH.

I CAN GIVE YOU SOME POINTERS ABOUT THE LAST TWO: WHERE YOU ARE AND HOW TO GO QUICKLY.

YOU'RE BEST SPEAKING TO LIZ KEOGH TO WORK OUT WHERE YOU WANT TO GO --

I HAVE ASKED LIZ TO JOIN US LATER.

LET'S START WITH WHERE YOU ARE NOW.

ON THE PHONE YOU SAID THAT YOU'RE SPENDING A LOT OF TIME ON GATHERING STATUS, BUT YOU STILL DO NOT KNOW WHERE YOU ARE.

YES.

THERE ARE ONLY THREE STATUSES FOR A TASK --

-- NOT STARTED --

-- WORK IN PROGRESS --

-- AND DONE.

72

PERCENTAGES ARE JUST NONSENSE. EVEN 99%.

THAT REMAINING PERCENT COULD TAKE WEEKS.

STILL A LOT OF UNCERTAINTY THERE.

FOR EACH STEP IN THE PROCESS OF WHAT YOU'RE DOING YOU NEED A QUEUE OR A BUFFER IN FRONT OF THEM FOR THE TASKS NOT STARTED YET.

BUT THAT SOUNDS LIKE EVEN MORE THAN I'M DOING NOW.

THEN GET THE TEAM TO DO IT FOR THEMSELVES.

THEY NEED TO KNOW WHAT'S GOING ON AFTER ALL.

B_ZZZT
B_ZZZT
B_ZZZT

BUT IT'S NOT FOR THEM. I NEED THE STATUS FOR MANAGEMENT.

IT'S MORE IMPORTANT THAT THE TEAM KNOWS THE STATUS THAN THAT MANAGEMENT DOES.

HIYA...

WHAT! ARE YOU CRAZY? WHY?!

SO THEY CAN CO-ORDINATE THEIR ACTIVITY.

BUT I DO THAT.

AND HOW IS THAT WORKING FOR YOU?

LET THE TEAM DO IT INSTEAD, SO YOU CAN FOCUS ON THE IMPORTANT STUFF.

I HAVE TO GO. I ASSUME YOU'LL BE OKAY HERE NOW.

YEAH. NO PROBLEM.

I'LL CALL TOMORROW.

HOW DO I DO THAT?

EVEN I STRUGGLE TO WORK MY WAY AROUND THE PLAN.

STICK YOUR WORK ON A WALL AND GET THEM TO UPDATE IT WITH YOU ONCE A DAY.

A FIVE OR TEN MINUTE MEETING SHOULD BE ENOUGH.

HOW DO I KEEP THE MEETING TO FIVE OR TEN MINUTES?

MAKE EVERYONE STAND UP.

OKAY. SO NOW I KNOW WHERE I AM --

-- HOW DO I GET TO GO AS QUICKLY AS POSSIBLE?

FIRST, FOCUS ON TIME RATHER THAN COST.

LEAVE THE DEVELOPERS AND TESTERS TO GET ON WITH THEIR TASKS.

YOUR JOB IS TO FOCUS ON BLOCKED ITEMS --

-- AND THE QUEUES OR 'WAITING' STATES,

MONITOR THAT PEOPLE ARE WORKING ON ONE ITEM AT A TIME --

-- PEOPLE WORKING ON MORE THAN ONE TASK MEANS YOU HAVE HIDDEN QUEUES.

75

LIZ, THIS IS LILLY'S SISTER, ROSE.

ROSE, THIS IS LIZ KEOGH.

HOW ARE YOU DOING?

GREAT. PLEASED TO MEET YOU.

I TAKE IT THAT JON HAS GOT THE BALL ROLLING --

-- WHERE ARE WE UP TO?

USING REAL OPTIONS TO HANDLE UNCERTAINTY.

AVOID COMMITTING TOO EARLY.

AND HOW DO YOU MANAGE THAT?

YOU HAVE SEVERAL WAYS OF DOING SOMETHING --

-- BUT DON'T KNOW THE 'BEST' WAY TO DO IT.

HAPPENS PRACTICALLY EVERY DAY.

RIGHT. THERE ARE THREE APPROACHES.

ONE, POSTPONE THE COMMITMENT, COLLECT MORE INFORMATION.

TWO, CHOOSE THE OPTION THAT IS EASIEST TO CHANGE.

IDEALLY YOU WOULD WANT TO HIRE SOMEONE LIKE HIM.

GARY...?

WHAT ARE YOU DOING HERE?

GARY? HE'S ON MY TEAM!

THIS IS THE LAST PLACE I WOULD EXPECT TO FIND YOU.

ROSE IS LILLY'S SISTER --

-- SHE NEEDS A REAL OPTIONS COACH.

YOU ARE KIDDING. STEVE IS GONNA FLIP.

ROSE, I THINK IT'S TIME FOR YOU TO BUY ME A DRINK.

FAIR ENOUGH. THIS ROUND'S ON ME.

I'LL GIVE YOU A HAND, AND WE CAN HAVE A CHAT.

78

Dear Susan,

At University most of my friends lived together in one of two big houses. They were on the same street side by side and they were owned by the same landlord. The landlord had a lot of properties that he rented out to students. All of them were the same. Same kitchen, same bathroom. I suspected the landlord had a warehouse full of spares that he bought at the same time he bought the kitchens.

I ate dinner at one of the houses quite a few times. I would come in and the kitchen would be spotless. Two of the guys in the house were really fussy and insisted on everyone cleaning up the kitchen after a meal. They were also pretty disciplined at replacing things that ran out. They had a schedule and everything. The others went along with it but I think they liked the place being tidy as well. Whenever I was there around dinner time they would offer something to eat. Within ten to fifteen minutes we would have something on our plates to eat. These were student days so it was normally pretty basic.

Next door were the gym guys. They had moved the kitchen table to one side and installed a weights bench. One thing I remember vividly was that there were never, ever, ever clean cups. The kitchen sink was normally full of dirty pots but a cup of tea required a trawl of the living room and residents bedrooms. Whenever I had a cup of tea there I normally had to go to the shops at the corner to get milk, tea bags and even washing up liquid on one occasion. It did not worry me too much as it took just as long to find a couple of cups in the rubbish tip that they called a living room. One time one of the guys invited a new girlfriend around for dinner. It took him so long to prepare it that she dumped him.

I've come to realise that technical debt is like a dirty kitchen. You cannot find anything and you have to clean up before you start to do any real work. While a little is still manageable on a daily basis, if it gets too big the act of cleaning up and hunting for things is a real gumption trap (from Zen and the Art of Motorcycle maintenance).
At some point the mess is too big to find things and it becomes easier to give up. This builds up to a series of failed attempts to clean up and the initiative to start becomes smaller and smaller.

Paying down technical debt or "Refactoring" as some of the developers call it is the equivalent of cleaning the kitchen and putting stuff in the right place. This means that the next person who comes along is able to find what they need where they expect it to be.

Options helped me realise that technical debt is not debt. It is not a fixed cost. Rather it is a sold option. The more valuable and urgent the requirement, the more the "sold option" (Technical Debt) costs you. As the guy who lost the girlfriend knows all too well. Sadly people never learn, he lost the next two girlfriends after me as well though we all became good friends.

I now realise that paying down technical debt is like keeping the kitchen clean. It helps me respond quicker and deliver faster with less effort. This gives me more options which is a good thing. Sometimes the most valuable investment for the business is a pair of technology cleaning gloves.

One last thing, tonight Lilly took me to The Learning Cantina. Amazing how she always finds these extraordinary places. She introduced me to Jon Terry and Liz Keogh and we had a great conversation about project management and Real Options. Sounds interesting, this options thinking. Made sense to me, but I'm not sure how this is going to help me. I'll first start with the project management ideas.

When I googled Liz I came across a blog post of hers describing a real life situation where she applied options thinking.

Good night, Susan. Time to get some sleep.

Liz Keogh's Blog

Software, Training, Coaching, Writing.

 July 01 Clients value changing their minds too

A few years back, I met Chris Parsons when he gave a talk about a topic I was hugely interested in. Chris was the CEO of Eden Development, a little software house down in Winchester. Meeting him resulted in us both appreciating offering options in real life.

After the talk Chris and I exchanged ideas about some questions he'd had difficulty answering. He seemed impressed and suggested I should come and coach his team for a day or two. I like small companies; they're usually fun and easy to coach. So, I offered him a fairly low rate and Chris replied promptly and said, "Come down on Monday."
"Hmmm, you said, 'A day or two.',", I reminded him. "You see, Winchester's two and a half hours by train, each way, and I don't really feel like travelling for five hours only to do it again the next day, so I have a proposal."

I offered Chris the option for my help on the second day, at the same low rate. Chris could buy this option for the price of a hotel and a meal. If he paid for my hotel, I'd stay there regardless. This way I would have a nice relaxed time instead of trying to travel there and back in one day, and if Chris wanted me back for the second day all he needed to do was let me know before I left on the first day.

Chris loved the idea. I booked the hotel, went there for my first day and started helping the team at Eden Development.

Chris Parsons was so pleased with the results on the first day that he asked me to come back on the second day - he used the option. When I came back in, Chris said, "I've spoken to our client and asked him to keep a prioritized list of the things he wants. We only need to know the top six things he wants us to work on. This allows us to help him focus on the stakeholder goals more effectively. We'll chat with him once a week to get more. Now...
how do we make this work?"

When I called back a few months later to see how things were going, they had reduced the limit to three items, talking to their client twice a week. It turned out their client loved having the option to change his mind too!

CHAPTER FOUR

Backlog | Prioritised | Ready for Analysis | Analysis | Ready for Dev | Development

NOW CAN YOU TAKE THESE ORANGE STICKIES AND PLACE THEM ON THOSE TASKS THAT ARE BLOCKED INDICATING WHY THEY ARE BLOCKED.

RIGHT....OKAY. AGAIN, LET'S STAND BACK AND HAVE A LOOK AT WHAT WE'VE GOT.

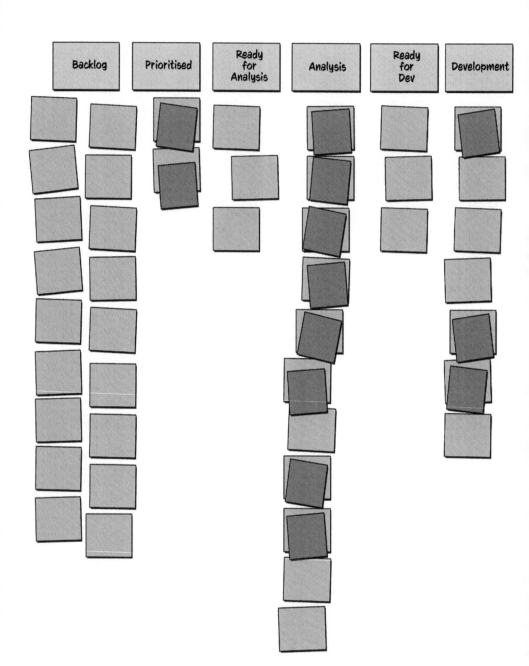

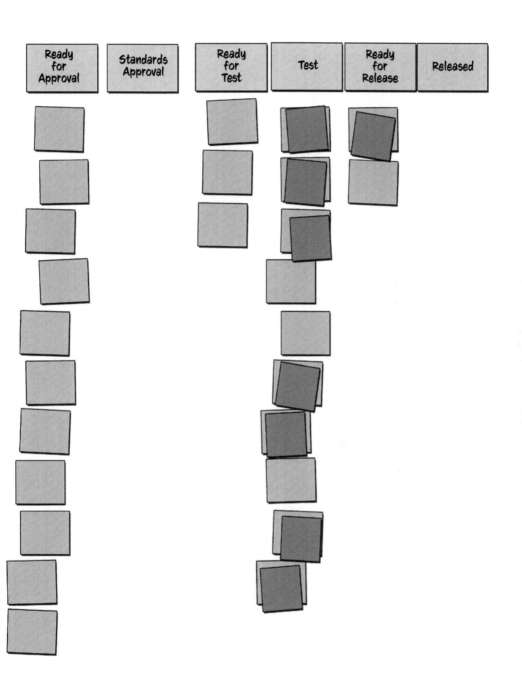

...A-HEM...

Backlog | Prioritised | for Analysis | for | Development | for Approval | Standards Approval | for Test | Test | for Release | Released

I CAN NOW SEE THAT WE CANNOT DELIVER THIS PLAN.

I CAN TELL THAT I HAVE BEEN FOCUSED ON GETTING YOU GUYS TO START THINGS --

-- AND WE'RE NOT GETTING THINGS FINISHED.

LET'S CHANGE THAT FOCUS TOWARDS FINISHING THINGS.

SO LET'S MOVE EVERYTHING THAT'S NOT BEING WORKED ON BACK TO THE 'READY FOR' STATE.

WHAT DO WE WORK ON FIRST?

THAT DEPENDS ON WHERE YOU WANT TO GO...

FOR NOW LET'S FOCUS ON COMPLETING WHAT WE STARTED AND WE CAN FIGURE OUT THE REST LATER.

91

YOU HATE HER MORE THAN ANYONE, GARY. WHAT'S GOING ON?

I THINK SHE IS TRYING TO CHANGE, STEVE.

SHE EVEN WENT TO TLC.

WE SHOULD GIVE HER A CHANCE.

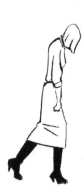

94

VISUALISATION BOARDS

3ᴿᴰ OCT

TODAY I WORKED WITH GARY ON CREATING A VISUALISATION BOARD FOR MY TEAM. BY VISUALISING OUR PROCESS AND MAKING THE PROCESS STEPS MORE EXPLICIT IT BECOMES EASIER FOR US TO SEE HOW WE ARE DOING AND WHERE THE PROBLEMS ARE.

WHAT IS A VISUALISATION BOARD?

A VISUALISATION BOARD IS A TOOL TO HELP YOU IMPROVE YOUR PROCESS. IT IS LITERALLY A BOARD WHERE YOU VISUALISE BOTH THE PROCESS AND ITS STEPS AND THE CURRENT STATUS OF WORK WITHIN THAT PROCESS.

ORIGINS OF A VISUALISATION BOARD

THE ORIGINS FOR A VISUALISATION BOARD IS AT TOYOTA. TOYOTA IDENTIFIED THAT STORING, TRUCKING, SHIPPING AND A NUMBER OF OTHER PROCESS STEPS IN THEIR MANUFACTURING PROCESS ARE NON VALUE ADDING. BY MAPPING OUT THE STEPS THAT CREATE VALUE AND THE STEPS IN-BETWEEN THAT DO NOT ADD VALUE YOU MAP THE 'VALUE STREAM'.

TAIICHI OHNO'S TOYOTA PRODUCTION SYSTEM FOCUSES ON THE DELIVERY OF VALUE AND THE CREATION OF KNOWLEDGE. IN LEAN THINKING (WRITTEN BY WOMACK AND JONES) THE PROCESS IS EXPLAINED BY GOING THROUGH THE DESCRIPTION OF THE VALUE STREAM OF A CAN OF COLA. THE VALUE OF A CAN OF COLA IS REALISED WHEN THE CAN IS CONSUMED.

THE VALUE STREAM OF A CAN OF COLA STARTS WITH THE EXTRACTION OF BAUXITE FROM A MINE IN AUSTRALIA. THE RESOURCES AND HALF-PRODUCTS ARE STORED, TRUCKED AND SHIPPED ALL OVER THE WORLD. IN ICELAND THE ORE IS USED TO PRODUCE INGOTS OF ALUMINIUM. IN FINLAND THE INGOTS ARE USED TO PRODUCE ROLLS OF ALUMINIUM. IN SPAIN THESE ALUMINIUM ROLLS ARE STAMPED INTO CIRCLES THAT ARE FORMED INTO CANS. THE CANS ARE FILLED WITH COLA, SEND TO THE WAREHOUSE AND FROM THERE TO SUPER-MARKETS WHERE WE BUY THEM AND FINALLY DRINK THE COLA. THE WHOLE PROCESS TAKES 365 DAYS HOWEVER THERE ARE ONLY 24 HOURS OF VALUE ADDING ACTIVITIES.

BY MAPPING THE PROCESS OUT IT BECOMES EASIER TO GET AN OVERVIEW OF WHAT IS HAPPENING. WE WANTED TO CREATE SOMETHING SIMILAR FOR OUR PROJECT. WHAT ARE ALL THE STEPS WE TAKE TO REALISE OUR GOAL AND HOW DO THEY ALL RELATE?

HOW TO CREATE A VISUALISATION BOARD?
WITH OUR PROJECT THE STEPS ARE LESS EXPLICIT AND LESS VISUAL. SO WE NEED TO DRAW THEM OUT. THE IMPORTANT VISUALISATION OF OUR BOARD IS BOTH THE STATES OF OUR WORK WHERE WE ADD VALUE AS WELL AS THE WAITING STATES OR QUEUES BEFORE AND AFTER THEM.

THE IDEAL VISUALISATION BOARD HAS ONLY THREE STATES.
"WAITING" (WORK IS WAITING TO BE DONE), "WORK IN PROGRESS" (WHERE WE DO THE ACTUAL WORK) AND "DONE" (WHEN THE WORK IS DONE, DUH). HOW- EVER IN THE REAL WORLD, SYSTEMS ARE OFTEN MORE COMPLICATED. THE WHOLE PROCESS CONSISTS OF MULTIPLE SPECIALISMS RESULTING IN MUL- TI-STEP PROCESSES. WE MODEL EACH OF THESE SPECIALISMS AS A COLUMN IN OUR VISUALISATION BOARD. IN ORDER TO CREATE A LITTLE BUFFER BETWEEN THESE STEPS THE VISUALISATION BOARD IS EXTENDED BY HAVING A "WAITING" AND "DONE" FOR EACH PROCESS STEP. AS THE "DONE" FROM ONE PROCESS IS THE "WAITING" OF THE NEXT PROCESS, THESE QUEUES ARE OFTEN NAMED AFTER THE PROCESS THEY FEED, E.G. "READY FOR DEVELOPMENT".

COLUMN MODELLING
STEPS TO CREATE A VISUALISATION BOARD TURNED OUT TO BE REASONABLY SIMPLE. WE MODELLED EACH STEP IN OUR PROCESS AS A COLUMN AND ADDED BUFFERS BETWEEN ALL THESE STEPS. WE TOOK EXTRA CARE TO ENSURE THAT ALL PROCESS STEPS DONE BY DIFFERENT INDIVIDUALS OR GROUPS ARE INCLUDED, EVEN THOUGH THEY MAY ONLY TAKE A FEW SECONDS.
AN EXAMPLE OF A STEP THAT COULD BE DONE QUICKLY BUT WE HAVE STILL MODELLED IS THE "STANDARDS APPROVAL" WHERE OUR SYSTEM ADMINISTRA- TORS CHECK IF EVERYTHING IS DONE ACCORDING TO THE STANDARDS. GETTING THE APPROVAL MAY SOMETIMES TAKE A LONG TIME AS THE ADMIN GUYS ARE GENERALLY VERY BUSY. THIS CAUSES US SIGNIFICANT DELAYS. BY HAVING THIS ON THE BOARD IT'S CLEARLY VISIBLE WHEN THIS IS DELAYING US.

HOPEFULLY WHEN THIS HAPPENS TOO OFTEN WE CAN HAVE A CONVERSATION ON HOW TO REMOVE THIS STEP AND KEEP EVERYBODY HAPPY AND SATISFIED. REMOVING THIS STEP IS NOT A PRIORITY JUST YET, WE WILL LOOK INTO IT WHEN WE HAVE SOME TIME TO SPARE. FIRST WE NEED TO CREATE TRUST IN EACH OTHER AND INCREASE THE VISIBILITY OF THE APPROVAL PROBLEM.

ARCHIVES

OCTOBER (1)

SEPTEMBER

(1)

AUGUST (0)

JULY (0)

JUNE (0)

MAY (1)

APRIL (0)

MARCH (0)

FEBRUARY (0)

JANUARY (1)

PREVIOUS
YEAR
(5)

PROCESS STEPS AND WAITING FOR THEM IS ONE TYPE OF QUEUE. THERE ARE TWO OTHER TYPES WE SHOULD LOOK OUT FOR: WAITING AND MULTITASKING.

WHEN WE CAN'T CONTINUE TO WORK ON SOMETHING BECAUSE WE HAVE TO WAIT ON SOMETHING OR SOMEONE, THE ITEMS WE CAN'T WORK ON AT THAT TIME ARE CONSIDERED BLOCKED.
TO VISUALISE THESE WE AGREED TO WRITE WHAT'S CAUSING THE DELAY ON A BRIGHTLY COLOURED STICKY NOTE. IF THE BOARD IS FULL OF THOSE BRIGHTLY COLOURED STICKIES WE KNOW WE HAVE A PROBLEM.

MULTITASKING IS WHEN SOMEONE WORKS ON MORE THAN ONE ITEM AT A TIME. WHEN YOU ARE WORKING ON MORE THAN ONE WORK ITEM, YOU HAVE CREATED A HIDDEN QUEUE FORMED BY THE ITEMS YOU ARE CURRENTLY NOT ACTIVELY WORKING ON. THE SOLUTION IS SIMPLE. FOR STARTERS WE DECIDED ON A ONE ITEM PER PERSON POLICY. WE'LL SEE HOW THIS WORKS OUT AND CAN CHANGE IT LATER.

BOTTLENECK / CAPACITY MANAGEMENT

ELI GOLDRATT CREATED A THEORY BASED ON IDENTIFYING THE CONSTRAINTS TO OPTIMISE THROUGHPUT IN A SYSTEM. IN OTHER WORDS HOW MUCH A FACTORY (OR ANY OTHER PROCESS) PRODUCES IS DETERMINED BY ITS SLOWEST STEP. ASSUME PRODUCING A CAR TAKES TEN STEPS. AT EACH OF THESE STEPS THE TEAM WORKING THERE IS ABLE TO HANDLE PRODUCING 20 CARS PER HOUR, EXCEPT FOR ONE STEP WHERE THEY CAN ONLY HANDLE PRODUCING 12 CARS PER HOUR. BECAUSE ALL OF THE STEPS HAVE TO BE DONE TO PRODUCE THE CAR, THE TOTAL PRODUCTIVITY CAN NEVER BE HIGHER THAN 12 CARS PER HOUR.

THE STEP THAT IS CREATING THE FEWEST CARS IN THIS EXAMPLE IS CALLED THE CONSTRAINT. IT CONSTRAINTS OR LIMITS THE TOTAL PRODUCTIVITY. ADDING ADDITIONAL CAPACITY TO ANYWHERE IN THE SYSTEM OTHER THAN AT THE CONSTRAINT WILL HAVE NO BENEFICIAL IMPACT. IT IS ONLY POSSIBLE TO IMPROVE THE WHOLE CAPACITY BY ADDING CAPACITY AT THE CONSTRAINT.

BOARD PATTERNS

GARY USED THIS THEORY OF CONSTRAINTS BY ELI GOLDRATT TO EXPLAIN SOME COMMON PATTERNS TO LOOK FOR WHEN USING A VISUALISATION BOARD. WHEN YOU HAVE A CONSTRAINT IN YOUR SYSTEM (BOARD) WORK WILL QUEUE UP IN FRONT OF A
CONSTRAINT. ALSO THE STEPS AFTER THE CONSTRAINT WILL HAVE LESS WORK READY TO WORK ON AS THEY ARE WAITING FOR WORK TO COME THROUGH THE CONSTRAINT.

ARCHIVES

OCTOBER (1)

SEPTEMBER (1)

AUGUST (0)

JULY (0)

JUNE (0)

MAY (1)

APRIL (0)

MARCH (0)

FEBRUARY (0)

JANUARY (1)

PREVIOUS YEAR
(5)

98

HEY, SIS. WHAT'S UP?

HOPE I'M NOT INTERRUPTING ANYTHING...

IT'S OKAY. I CAN MULTITASK.

WE'RE HAVING SOME TROUBLE WITH THE TESTING. DETAILING SPECIFICATIONS.

DO YOU KNOW ANYONE THAT CAN BE ANY HELP WITH BUSINESS ANALYSIS?

A FEW. I TAKE IT THAT THIS IS A, 'AS SOON AS POSSIBLE' SITUATION?

ISN'T IT ALWAYS?

HANG ON A MO... PUTTING YOU ON SPEAKER.

BRRHGG BRRHGG

LILLY...

HEY, MAGNUS. HOW'S IT GOING?

SAME AS USUAL.

THAT BAD, HUH?

BRRHGG BRR EHKK

YOU KNOW IT.

HEH. I'VE GOT MY SISTER, ROSE, PATCHED IN. SHE'S IN DESPERATE NEED OF A BUSINESS ANALYST --

-- AND AS YOU'RE THE MAN TO GO TO IN A CRISIS, I'D THOUGHT I'D GIVE YOU FIRST CRACK AT BEING HER WHITE KNIGHT.

ALWAYS WELCOME THE OPPORTUNITY TO RESCUE A DAMSEL IN DISTRESS.

ROSE, THIS IS MAGNUS.

HIYA.

MAGNUS, THIS IS MY BIG SISTER, ROSE.

HELLO, ROSE.

RIGHT. NOW THAT I'VE INTRODUCED YOU, I'M GOING TO LEAVE YOU KIDS TO IT. I'LL SPEAK TO YOU GUYS LATER. PLAY NICE.

THANKS, SIS.

A PLEASURE AS ALWAYS, LILLY.

SO TELL ME, ROSE, JUST HOW DESPERATE IS THE SITUATION?

101

THANK YOU FOR MEETING US AT SUCH SHORT NOTICE.

MY PLEASURE.

OUR TESTERS DO NOT KNOW WHAT TO TEST.

SO WHAT DO YOU THINK THE PROBLEM IS?

OKAY. LET'S APPROACH THIS FROM ANOTHER PERSPECTIVE --

-- WHAT DO YOU WANT TO DO?

DELIVER THE SOFTWARE THE CLIENTS ASK FOR.

NO.

YOU WANT TO DELIVER VALUE.

EVEN MORE SO, YOU WANT TO DELIVER IT IN SMALL SLICES.

WHY SMALL SLICES?

THEN THE CLIENTS CAN SEE EXACTLY WHAT THEY ARE GETTING, AND IF NECESSARY ADJUST.

ALSO THEY CAN PUT IT INTO THE MARKET AND GET FEEDBACK ON IT FROM CUSTOMERS OR POTENTIAL CUSTOMERS.

YOU KNOW WHAT YOU HAVE JUST DONE?

??

YOU HAVE ASKED FOR A CUP OF TEA.

YOU DIDN'T ASK FOR A TEA BAG.

I ASKED FOR SOMETHING OF VALUE TO ME.

EXACTLY.

YOUR CLIENTS ASK FOR A TEA BAG LIKE THIS ONE --

-- WHAT THEY REALLY WANT IS A HOT CUP OF TEA.

I GET IT.

THEN THEY COME BACK FOR MILK, A CUP, HOT WATER, ETC.

RIGHT ON.

SO HOW DO I FIND OUT WHAT THE VALUE IS?

WHERE IS THE VALUE IN ANY SYSTEM?

THE INPUTS OR THE OUTPUTS?

THE OUTPUTS, I SUPPOSE.

WRONG.

IT'S IN THE OUTCOMES WHICH ARE RESULTS OF THE OUTPUTS.

SO WHAT USE IS THAT?

IT MEANS THAT IF THE CLIENT IS DESCRIBING THE INPUTS OR OPERATIONS OF THE SYSTEM, YOU HAVE TO FIND THE OUTCOME THEY NEED TO IDENTIFY THE VALUE.

HOW DO I DO THAT?

ASK 'WHY' TO MOVE THE DISCUSSION IN THE DIRECTION OF THE OUTCOMES.

IS THAT ALL?

WELL, YOU NEED TO KNOW WHEN TO STOP ASKING 'WHY?'.

YOU CAN ONLY DO THAT IF YOU KNOW WHAT BUSINESS VALUE LOOKS LIKE.

-- IT'S INCREASING REVENUE OR REDUCING COSTS.

HERE YOU GO.

THAT'S OBVIOUS --

THANKS.

THANK YOU.

WELL THINK BACK...

WHEN HAVE YOU AS A HUMAN BEING KNOWN THAT YOU HAVE DELIVERED VALUE TO SOMEONE ELSE?

THERE ARE A NUMBER OF WAYS.

SOMETIMES THEY TELL YOU, BUT THAT IS RARE.

SOMETIMES IT'S BECAUSE THEY START TO USE WHAT YOU HAVE DELIVERED.

AND YOU'LL NOTICE THEY'LL START ASKING DIFFERENT KINDS OF QUESTIONS.

OKAY. WHAT NEXT?

GOING BACK TO THE CUP OF TEA: SO NOW WE KNOW WE WANT A TASTY HOT DRINK RATHER THAN A TEA BAG.

WE HAVE MORE OPTIONS IN THE WAY WE CAN DELIVER THE VALUE.

SO LET'S ASSUME I STILL WANT A CUP OF TEA.

NOW THAT WE KNOW YOU WANT A CUP OF TEA, WE CAN EASILY WORK BACKWARDS TO IDENTIFY THE PROCESSES AND INPUTS NEEDED TO PRODUCE A CUP OF TEA.

SO WE NEED A TEA BAG, A CUP, MILK, SUGAR AND A SPOON.

HOW DO WE GET HOT WATER?

WE NEED COLD WATER THAT WE HEAT IN A KETTLE.

I AGREE WE NEED COLD WATER --

-- BUT DEPENDING ON YOUR CONTEXT, THERE ARE MANY WAYS TO HEAT WATER.

FOR EXAMPLE, ON A CAMPING TRIP YOU MAY HEAT WATER ON A FIRE OR EVEN TAKE IT IN A FLASK.

ALSO YOU SAID YOU NEED A TEA BAG.

WHAT WOULD YOU NEED A TEA BAG FOR?

TO EXTRACT TEA.

SO DO YOU NEED A TEA BAG?

HMMMM.

I THINK I JUST NEED DRY TEA LEAVES AND A WAY OF FILTERING THEM FROM THE WATER.

SO BY STARTING AT THE END I CAN MORE EASILY SEE ASSUMPTIONS I'M MAKING AND THUS SPOT MORE OPTIONS TO DELIVER WHAT IS NEEDED.

WHAT IF I MISS SOMETHING?

THE GREAT THING ABOUT STARTING AT THE END IS THAT YOU CANNOT MISS SOMETHING THAT IS NEEDED TO PRODUCE THE OUTCOME.

NOT ONLY THAT, BUT YOU DO NOT INCLUDE THINGS THAT ARE UNNECESSARY.

SO THE BUSINESS VALUE DEFINES THE SCOPE OF THE FUNCTIONALITY?

AND YOUR STRATEGY DETERMINES WHAT VALUE YOU ARE NOT CURRENTLY GOING TO CHASE.

YES.

COOL.

AS A RESULT YOU CAN DELIVER WITH THE MINIMAL AMOUNT OF EFFORT BY CHOOSING APPROPRIATE OPTIONS TO IMPLEMENT.

WHAT DO YOU MEAN?

SAY YOU ARE SETTING UP A CAFÉ ON THE BEACH --

-- YOU START BY USING FLASKS OF HOT WATER TO TEST THE MARKET.

THEN YOU BOIL WATER ON A CAMPING GAS RING --

-- AND EVENTUALLY PAY FOR AN ELECTRICITY SUPPLY.

IS THAT IT?

WE HAVE DONE IT FOR TEA.

AND FROM HERE YOU WOULD LOOK AT THE REST OF THE SOLUTION.

MEANING?

WE NEED TO CONSIDER IF THERE ARE OTHER EXAMPLES THAT REQUIRE US TO CHANGE OUR SOLUTION --

-- OR 'BREAK THE MODEL' AS WE CALL IT.

WHAT DO YOU MEAN?

IF WE WANT TO SELL COFFEE, THINGS CAN REMAIN THE SAME.

HOWEVER, IF WE WANT TO SELL CANS OF SODA WE WOULD NEED TO HAVE SOMETHING THAT COOLS STUFF.

ALL CANS OF SODA WOULD BE THE SAME.

AND ICE CREAMS, WE NEED TO KEEP THEM FROZEN.

ONCE AGAIN, ALL ICE CREAMS WOULD BE THE SAME.

I STILL DON'T GET IT.

LET ME DO THIS WITH AN ABSTRACT EXAMPLE.

110

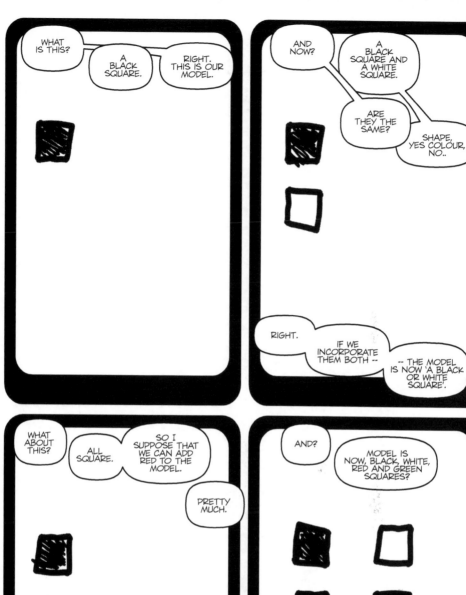

113

Blobs

RANDOM MUSINGS - LILLY RANDALL

Hunt the value

Always looking for ways of analysing problems to come up with solutions I came across a website that described Feature Injection. Feature Injection has three steps that you continuously loop through:

1) Hunt the value.
2) Inject the features.
3) Break the model.

What value to hunt?

Feature Injection tells us to move toward the outcome until we encounter value. That sounds nice, but is more difficult when you try to apply this. Value is created when a benefit is created for either the consumer or the producer of a product or service that they are willing to pay for.

There are four ways of generating value: increasing or protecting revenue, or reducing or avoiding costs in alignment with the strategy of the organisation.

If that is the case then why are Twitter and Instagram worth so much? Facebook bought Instagram for a cool billion dollars even though it does not generate a cent in revenue. Twitter was worth gazzilions even when it wasn't generating any revenue either. The value model is well and truly broken!

A number of modern companies do not build revenue models. Instead they build options to generate revenue. These options have two important aspects.... Network and Usage.

Recent Posts

October (4)

September (5)

August (3)

July (4)

June (5)

May (5)

April (4)

March (5)

February (3)

January (6)

Previous Year
(63)

Network

Social Networks are more valuable to their users if they have more users or a bigger network. How much is the first telephone worth if no one else in the world has one? Only Alexander Graham Bell really got to think about that and came up with a clever solution. He understood the importance of a network and gave away phones for free to hotels and other places where many people would get to use them.

Usage

Usage is another important aspect. If people do not use your service, there is no way you generate revenue from them. The more they use your service, the more likely they are to generate a revenue for you. This revenue can be from your users paying for your service or can be generated indirectly by placing ads in front of your customers.

There's value in numbers

In order to get the most value out of the network and usage it is important to accurately measure EVERYTHING! Thinking you have a big network is not the same as knowing you have exactly 501,217 users and seeing a graph of the trend. Thinking people use your product is not the same as knowing that they use it on average for 27 minutes per day. Numbers are key!

Hunting the value requires you to think about your context and where the value could be. It is no longer just reducing cost and increasing revenue. Understand where your value is coming from.

Seeya next time -
L

Dear Susan,

Really excited about some stuff at work. Last week we met with Magnus (a friend of Lilly) who explained "Feature Injection" to Kent and me. This week we started applying it together with the team.

What we discovered was that much of the work we were doing so far was building Tea Bags when in fact we wanted to deliver cups of tea. We needed to become more focused on the end result, not just doing the steps.

For each task (or tea bag as we now call them) we identified the value it delivers. It turned out that a lot of the items we were working on were related to the same outcome and that we should be doing them together to deliver value rather than simply deliver unrelated chunks of functionality.

We called a meeting with our customers and asked them to tell us what they wanted. Rather than discuss the individual Tea Bags, we discussed the value items or cups of tea. It was a really hard discussion but we managed to defer a number of items. Even more amazing was that for two value items the customers decided the value did not justify the effort required and so we scrapped them altogether.

We have agreed a regular meeting every two weeks to prioritise the next thing we want to start. So it would appear that one of the key benefits of Feature Injection is not just to identify the things needed but to identify the things we should start building.

You know what Susan, I may just start to like running a project (but don't tell any one).

Good night,
Rose

CHAPTER FIVE

120

122

DEPENDS ON WHO IT IS --

BUT I THINK THAT I COULD COACH AND PAIR WITH THEM FOR A WEEK TO GET THEM UP TO SPEED.

THAT'S A BIT MORE REASONABLE, ISN'T IT?

WON'T THAT CAUSE A DELAY IF KENT ISN'T FOCUSED?

NOT REALLY. I COULD ALWAYS BE AVAILABLE IF NEEDED.

THAT'S THE GOOD THING ABOUT NOT HAVING ME COMMITED TO AN ACTUAL TASK.

IF SOMEONE NEEDS ME FOR COACHING OR REMOVING A BLOCK, MY TASK WILL NOT END UP BEING LATE.

AND THAT'S HOW WE'VE BEEN RUNNING IT EVER SINCE.

WE ALLOCATE THE PEOPLE WITH THE MOST OPTIONS LAST.

THAT ALLOWS US THE MOST FLEXIBILITY TO DEAL WITH ANY SITUATION THAT COMES UP.

I ALWAYS HAVE GARY AVAILABLE TO FIX PROBLEMS OR HELP OTHERS.

SO YOU ALLOCATE THE MOST EXPERIENCED PEOPLE LAST?

PARTLY.

EXPERIENCED PEOPLE HAVE MOST OPTIONS.

HOWEVER, SOME EXPERTS CAN, OR WILL, ONLY WORK ON ONE TYPE OF TASK.

SO YOU DECIDE WHAT PEOPLE WILL WORK BASED ON EXPERIENCE?

IT'S MORE DYNAMIC THAN THAT.

THE TEAM SELF ALLOCATES TO CONSTRAINTS.

WHAT IS A CONSTRAINT?

A CONSTRAINT IS ANYTHING THAT PREVENTS US FROM REACHING OUR OBJECTIVE.

WE RAN INTO SUCH A PROBLEM TWO MONTHS AGO.

WE HAVE A PROBLEM --

-- ONE DAY WE NEED MORE ANALYSTS. THE NEXT DAY WE NEED MORE TESTERS.

THE CONSTRAINT KEEPS MOVING.

WELL THAT'S NOT EXACTLY HELPFUL IS IT?

ANY IDEAS?

128

IMAGINE THE INFORMATION IS SOME ROPE BEING PULLED THROUGH A HOLE OF EXACTLY THE SAME WIDTH.

THIS IS ANALYSIS, TEST PLAN AND TEST EXECUTION.

WHEN BUGS ARE DETECTED, THAT INFORMATION THEN GOES BACKWARDS INTO DEVELOPMENT --

-- AND THEN FORWARD AGAIN INTO TEST EXECUTION.

BUT BECAUSE THE ROPE IS THE SAME THICKNESS IT BECOMES DIFFICULT TO MANAGE BOTH STREAMS AT THE SAME TIME.

CAN'T YOU JUST USE A THINNER ROPE?

THAT'S NOT REALLY THE BEST WAY.

IT'S THE SAME AS SPLITTING THE RESOURCES INTO TWO GROUPS.

THE SECOND ONE DEVOTED TO FINDING THE BUGS.

ANOTHER WAY IS TO WORK FOR A BIT, SORT OUT ANY BUGS, WORK FOR A BIT MORE, SORT OUT ANY BUGS, ETC.

SWITCHING BETWEEN THE VARIOUS TASKS UNTIL THE JOB IS DONE.

SO THESE BUGS DISRUPT THE FLOW OF DEVELOPMENT.

SO WHAT'S THE SOLUTION?

GLAD YOU ASKED!!

IF WE MOVE ANALYSIS AND TEST PLANNING TO BE PARALLEL TO EACH OTHER AND HAVE ANALYSTS AND TESTERS COLLABORATE --

ANALYSIS ⟷ TEST PLAN

DEVELOPMENT

TEST EXECUTION

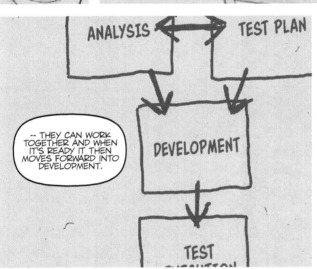

ANALYSIS ⟷ TEST PLAN

DEVELOPMENT

TEST EXECUTION

-- THEY CAN WORK TOGETHER AND WHEN IT'S READY IT THEN MOVES FORWARD INTO DEVELOPMENT.

IT MAY TAKE A BIT MORE TIME TO GET TO THE DEVELOPMENT BUT IT DOES REMOVE ANY DUPLICATION OR WASTE.

WELL, THAT DOES MAKE SOME SENSE.

LET'S GO THROUGH IT ONE MORE TIME BEFORE EXPLAINING IT TO THE TEAM.

131

THANK YOU.

I HAVE SOME SERIOUS CONCERNS ABOUT ROSE.

GO AHEAD.

ROSE HAS JUST ASKED FOR TWO JUNIOR PEOPLE AND OFFERED TWO EXPERIENCED PEOPLE IN EXCHANGE.

WHAT IS THE PROBLEM?

I THINK SHE WANTS PEOPLE SHE CAN MANAGE AND STRUGGLES WITH EXPERIENCED PEOPLE.

SHE'S CLEARLY NOT COMPETENT TO RUN THIS PROJECT.

OKAY.

WHAT DO YOU THINK?

LET'S SEND DUNCAN IN TO REVIEW WHAT SHE IS DOING.

AND?

AND IF THERE IS A PROBLEM WE WILL SHUT THEM DOWN.

WHO?

ALL OF THEM.

STAFF LIQUIDITY

15TH DEC

THERE IS VALUE IN SHORTER ITERATIONS OF DEVELOPMENT. LONGER ITERA-
TIONS ARE RISKIER TO THE BUSINESS INVESTOR WHO IS FUNDING THE PROJECT,
BECAUSE SHORTER ITERATIONS PROVIDE THE INVESTOR WITH MORE OPTIONS.
AND MORE OPTIONS MEANS MORE WAYS TO CONTROL THE PROJECT AND
MANAGE THE RISKS. THIS BLOG POST EXPLAINS HOW TO ACHIEVE A HIGH STAFF
LIQUIDITY TO ENABLE THIS BUSINESS FLEXIBILITY.

IMAGINE A PROJECT WHERE THE INVESTOR IS PREPARED TO FUND A YEAR OF
DEVELOPMENT OF THE PROJECT. AT THE EXTREME THE PROJECT COULD
EITHER DO ONE ITERATION AND ATTEMPT TO DELIVER THE PERFECT PRODUCT
OR SERVICE AFTER A YEAR.
ALTERNATIVELY, THEY COULD CREATE A NEW WORKING VERSION OF THE PROD-
UCT EVERY MONTH, MEANING TWELVE ITERATIONS. *

MANAGING DELIVERY RISK

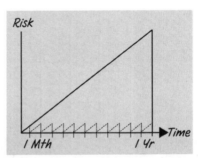

IN THIS DIAGRAM THE SOLID LINE REPRESENTS THE DELIVERY RISK FOR THE
SITUATION WHERE THERE IS ONE ITERATION. AS THE INVESTOR KEEPS INVEST-
ING MONEY AND GETS NOTHING IN RETURN HIS RISK CONTINUOUSLY GOES UP.
WHEN THE PROJECT DELIVERS THE RISK GOES DOWN.
THE DOTTED LINE REPRESENTS THE TWELVE ITERATIONS APPROACH. THE
INVESTOR STILL INVESTS CONTINUOUSLY, BUT AT EACH DELIVERY HIS RISK GOES
DOWN AS HE SEES THE RESULTS AND HAS THE OPPORTUNITY TO CHANGE
DIRECTION.**

FOR THE ONE ITERATION PROJECT, THE INVESTOR CONTINUES TO INVEST AND
ONLY FINDS OUT WHERE THEY TRULY ARE WHEN THE PROJECT DELIVERS AFTER
ONE YEAR.

FOR THE TWELVE ITERATION PROJECT, THE INVESTOR FINDS OUT WHERE THEY ARE AT ELEVEN POINTS PRIOR TO THE "FINAL" DELIVERY.

WHICH PROJECT WOULD YOU RATHER INVEST IN?

FLEXIBLE PROJECTS

THE PROJECT WITH TWELVE ITERATIONS IS SIGNIFICANTLY LESS RISKY BECAUSE THE INVESTOR HAS THE FOLLOWING OPTIONS.

1. STOP INVESTING IF THE PROJECT IS NOT MAKING THE EXPECTED PROGRESS.
2. STOP INVESTING IF THE PROJECT DELIVERS THE VALUE EARLY.
3. INCREASE INVESTMENT IF THE PROJECT IS MORE SUCCESSFUL THAN ORIGINALLY THOUGHT.
4. CHANGE DIRECTION OF THE PROJECT AS THEY COLLECT FEEDBACK FROM THEIR USERS / MARKET.

IN ORDER TO TAKE ADVANTAGE OF THESE OPTIONS, THE INVESTOR NEEDS TO BE ABLE TO CHANGE DIRECTION QUICKLY. ONE OF THE HARDEST ASPECTS IN THIS IS THE STAFFING. DEPENDING ON WHETHER THE FUNDING IS INCREASED OR DECREASED STAFF NEEDS TO BE EITHER ADDED TO THE PROJECT OR REMOVED.
IN MANY ORGANIZATIONS IT CAN TAKE SEVERAL MONTHS TO EFFECTIVELY SCALE A PROJECT UP OR DOWN. IN THIS PERIOD THE OPPORTUNITY FOR THIS PROJECT MAY HAVE BEEN LOST OR A COMPETITOR HAS ALREADY FILLED THE SPOT.

WE MEASURE THIS TIMING GAP AS STAFF LIQUIDITY. STAFF LIQUIDITY IS MEASURED AS THE TIME IT TAKES FROM WHEN THE INITIAL INVESTMENT IS APPROVED TO HAVING A FULLY GELLED AND FULLY UP TO SPEED TEAM WORKING ON THE PROJECT. A LOW LIQUIDITY MEANS IT IS HARD TO MOVE STAFF AROUND ON PROJECTS, WHEREAS A HIGH LIQUIDITY MEANS IT IS EASY TO RAMP PROJECTS UP AND DOWN AND DO SO QUICKLY. THIS APPLIES TO THE INITIAL INVESTMENT AS WELL AS ANY INCREMENTAL INVESTMENTS.

IN OTHER WORDS STAFF LIQUIDITY IS THE TIME NEEDED TO:

1. APPROVE AND HIRE STAFF.
2. GEL THE TEAM.
3. TRAIN THE TEAM.

ARCHIVES

DECEMBER (2)

NOVEMBER (1)

OCTOBER (1)

SEPTEMBER (1)

AUGUST (0)

JULY (0)

JUNE (0)

MAY (1)

APRIL (0)

MARCH (0)

FEBRUARY (0)

JANUARY (1)

PREVIOUS YEAR (5)

HOW TO ACHIEVE HIGH STAFF LIQUIDITY

ACHIEVING HIGH STAFF LIQUIDITY REQUIRES DELIBERATE MANAGEMENT. IT DOES NOT HAPPEN BY ACCIDENT. WE CREATE HIGH STAFF LIQUIDITY AS FOLLOWS:
1) NO KEY MAN DEPENDENCIES ON A PROJECT.
2) ALLOCATE STAFF WITH THE FEWEST OPTIONS FIRST, STAFF WITH MOST OPTIONS LAST.
3) LET STAFF WITH MOST OPTIONS COACH AND HELP THE STAFF WITH THE LEAST OPTIONS.

STAFF LIQUIDITY IS ANOTHER NAME FOR HAVING OPTIONS ABOUT HOW YOU DEPLOY YOUR STAFF.

1. KEY MAN DEPENDENCIES. KEY MAN DEPENDENCY IS A MEASUREMENT OF HOW DEPENDENT AN ORGANIZATION IS ON SPECIFIC PEOPLE. THESE PEOPLE HAVE SPECIFIC KNOWLEDGE THAT IS NOT SHARED WITH OTHERS. IF THEY QUIT OR IF SOMETHING BAD HAPPENS TO THEM THE ORGANIZATION IS IN SERIOUS TROUBLE.

THE RISK MANAGER FOR THE ORGANIZATION SHOULD ENSURE THAT ALL DEPARTMENTS AND GROUPS ARE AWARE OF THEIR KEY MAN DEPENDENCIES AND MANAGE THEM. MANAGING THE DEPENDENCIES PROPERLY ENSURES THE ORGANIZATION HAS REAL OPTIONS, THAT THE ORGANIZATION HAS MORE THAN ONE OR TWO PEOPLE WHO CAN PERFORM EACH FUNCTION WITHIN THE ORGANIZATION OR GROUP. MANAGING THIS IS SIMPLE.

EACH ORGANIZATION OR GROUP CREATES A GRID WITH STAFF NAMES ACROSS THE TOP AND FUNCTIONS DOWN THE SIDE. EACH PERSON GRADES HIMSELF FOR EACH FUNCTION.

"1" MEANS THEY CAN PERFORM THE BASICS OF THE FUNCTION.
"2" MEANS THEY CAN PERFORM THE FUNCTION ADEQUATELY.
"3" MEANS THE FUNCTION HAS NO SECRETS TO THEM.

ANY FUNCTION WITH THREE OR MORE PEOPLE AT LEVEL "3" IS "GREEN" OR "SAFE". ANY FUNCTION WITH TWO PEOPLE AT LEVEL "3" IS "YELLOW" OR "AT RISK". ANY FUNCTION WITH ONE OR NO PEOPLE AT LEVEL "3" IS "RISK". HERE IS AN EXAMPLE MATRIX:

	Status	Tom	Dick	Harriot	Jones
Sales	Green	3	3	3	2
Payroll	Red	3	2	1	0
Delivery	Yellow	3	3	2	2

ARCHIVES

DECEMBER (2)

NOVEMBER (1)

OCTOBER (1)

SEPTEMBER (1)

AUGUST (0)

JULY (0)

JUNE (0)

MAY (1)

APRIL (0)

MARCH (0)

FEBRUARY (0)

JANUARY (1)

PREVIOUS YEAR (5)

THE RISK MANAGER ASKS THE DEPARTMENTS TO ASSESS THE RISK ON A
REGULAR BASIS (E.G. BI-MONTHLY) AND TRACK THE CHANGES. ONE OTHER
IMPORTANT FACTOR IS HOW LONG IT TAKES TO TRAIN A PERSON IN A FUNC-
TION. FUNCTIONS THAT TAKE LONGER TO TRAIN ARE RISKIER THAN THOSE
THAT CAN BE TAUGHT QUICKLY.

2. ALLOCATE STAFF. ALLOCATE STAFF WITH THE FEWEST OPTIONS FIRST. IN
THE ABOVE DEPARTMENT, JONES WOULD BE ALLOCATED FIRST. HE HAS THE
LEAST EXPERIENCE. PLACING HIM IN ONE OF THE AREAS HE HAS SOME EXPERI-
ENCE IN ALLOWS HIM TO IMPROVE HIS KNOWLEDGE AND BECOME LEVEL "3"
OVER TIME. HARRIOT WOULD BE ALLOCATED NEXT. SHE WOULD PROBABLY BE
ALLOCATED TO "DELIVERY" TO STRETCH HER. DICK WOULD BE ALLOCATED
NEXT. HE WOULD BE ON "PAYROLL".

3. LET MOST EXPERIENCED STAFF COACH. TOM WOULD NOT BE ALLOCATED
ANY RESPONSIBILITIES. HE SHOULD ASSIST THE OTHERS EITHER BY TRAINING,
COACHING OR OTHERWISE HELPING THEM. IF ANY ISSUE ARISES, HE IS
INSTANTLY AVAILABLE TO ADDRESS THE ISSUE. IN ORDER TO PROTECT OUR
LIQUIDITY, TOM ADDRESSES THE ISSUE WITH DICK, HARRIOT OR JONES SO THAT
ONCE THE SOLUTION IS IDENTIFIED THEY TAKE THE RESPONSIBILITY FOR IT, AND
THEY FREE TOM UP TO BE INSTANTLY AVAILABLE TO ADDRESS THE NEXT HIGH
PRIORITY ISSUE.

THE ROLE OF MANAGEMENT IS TO MANAGE THE LIQUIDITY OF THEIR AREA OF
RESPONSIBILITY. IDEALLY THE TEAM SELF MANAGES THEIR LIQUIDITY BUT IN
THE EVENT THAT THEY DO NOT, RESPONSIBILITY LIES WITH THE MANAGER. THIS
IS PARTICULARLY THE CASE AS SOME TEAM MEMBERS MAY MAKE IT HARD FOR
OTHERS TO LEARN WHAT THEY KNOW AS THEY MAY ACTUALLY PREFER TO
REMAIN THE KEY MAN IN ORDER TO IMPROVE THEIR JOB SECURITY.

HOW LIQUID DO YOU NEED TO BE?
LIKE FINANCIAL MARKETS LIQUIDITY DOES NOT MEAN THE ENTIRE ORGANIZA-
TION NEEDS THE ABILITY TO MOVE TO A DIFFERENT
PROJECT IMMEDIATELY. INSTEAD A SMALL FRACTION (5 - 10%) SHOULD BE
LIQUID. THIS IS SUFFICIENT TO RESPOND QUICKLY AND GET THE REST UP TO
SPEED LATER.
HOWEVER THE ACT OF STAFFING A NEW PROJECT OR INCREASING INVESTMENT
IN AN EXISTING ONE REDUCES THE LIQUIDITY OF THE ORGANIZATION AT THAT
TIME. ACTION NEEDS TO BE TAKEN TO FREE UP THIS LIQUIDITY AS SOON AS
POSSIBLE IN ORDER TO BE ABLE TO RESPOND TO THE NEXT SITUATION JUST AS
QUICKLY.

** THANK YOU TO KEVIN TATE FOR SHARING THIS DIAGRAM.

CHAPTER SIX

140

NO, NO. IT'S NOT LIKE THAT.

THIS IS PURELY AN INFORMATION GATHERING EXERCISE.

WE'VE HEARD A FEW THINGS AND WE WANT YOU TO GO IN, HAVE A LOOK AROUND --

-- AND WE NEED TO SEE WHAT HAS TO BE DONE.

REALLY?

ARE YOU SURE I'M THE RIGHT PERSON FOR THIS?

I'VE GOT MY OWN PROJECT TO LOOK AFTER.

WE APPRECIATE THAT, BUT THIS PROJECT'S HAD A BIT OF A TROUBLED HISTORY --

-- AND WE NEED TO SEE WHAT HAS TO BE DONE.

WE TRUST YOU. YOU'LL KNOW WHAT TO LOOK FOR.

WHAT PROJECT IS IT?

ROSE. ON THE SECOND FLOOR.

HER?

I THOUGHT SHE WAS ALL RIGHT.

SHE WAS DOING ALL RIGHT.

LIKE WE SAID, THIS IS JUST FOR INFORMATION.

IF THE PROJECT FAILS, IT CAN HAVE SERIOUS IMPLICATIONS FOR THE COMPANY.

WE JUST NEED TO MAKE SURE WE DO THE RIGHT THING.

OKAY.

I'LL CHECK HER OUT.

141

144

Dear Susan,

I always thought Game Theory was something for the geeks in the maths and computing department. I never realised that it applied to real life and that it was useful to understand how groups work.

The Prisoner's Dilemma is the most popular game to explain Game Theory. In the Prisoner's Dilemma, two men are arrested for the same crime. The sentence they receive depends on whether they testify against the other person and whether the other person testifies against them. The sentences are:

Neither prisoner testifies: One year for each prisoner.

Both prisoners testify: Two years for each prisoner.

One testifies and the other does not: the prisoner who testifies gets no sentence and the other gets three years.

Obviously the best outcome is to testify against the other prisoner in the hope he does not testify. If the game is played over and over again in an "infinite" game this can lead to both players testifying each go. As a result the system has failed as both players get two years each go.

In the 1960s, the American Department of Defence commissioned Thomas Schelling to come up with a Game Theory Strategy to defeat the Soviet Union. He developed the Strategy of Conflict. The main aspect of the Strategy of Conflict is to withhold information and not allow the competition to negotiate directly with the decision maker. The Strategy of Conflict is the best strategy to optimise an individual's performance before the system fails.

After the system fails, the participants start to collaborate. The main aspect of collaboration is information sharing.

Let's consider a group's dynamics in the context of Game Theory. As a group comes together, each member of the group withholds information and tries to win, or to put it another way, they adopt the Strategy of Conflict. As this behaviour continues, conflict starts to occur as members in the group start to fail. Eventually a member fails catastrophically which causes the group to fail. After the group failure, members start to share information with each other.

Eventually the group becomes effective at making sure each member has the information they need to make the best decision. Another way of looking at this is that the group goes through the stages of forming, storming, (failure), norming, performing. I consider this sequence, known as the Tuckman Model of Group Performance, as inevitable for group development.

From Real Options, we know that people's behaviour shows that their preference is "Being Right", "Being Wrong" and then "Being Uncertain". This means that if we can insert enough uncertainty, the group will perceive the situation as failing and tip into collaboration. On a cautionary note, a group that is collaborating will tip into conflict if there is too much uncertainty for a sustained period. Managers engaging in reorganisations may be advised to take heed of this point. A reorganisation done slowly is more damaging than one done quickly as it will damage collaboration.

Another important lesson from this model is that anyone who bans or suppresses conflict prevents healthy group development. In fact, accelerating conflict and making it occur earlier will mean that the group progresses earlier and engages in smaller conflicts rather than bigger conflicts that are caused by suppressed feelings. The team develops conflict resolution skills rather than conflict avoidance. I find that humor and making fun of people are powerful tools for this. Done with care it creates small conflicts and it allows the team to practice their collaboration and conflict resolution skills as a team.

A final thought before I hit the sack. The opposite of a good relationship is not a bad relationship, it is no relationship. The thing I now look for on the team are those people who do not communicate with each other. Once I've spotted a lack of communication, there are a million strategies for getting someone to communicate. This non-communication is often the direct result of a culture of conflict avoidance where people are not allowed to engage in an argument. People who hide things under the table are only doing themselves a favor and at the same time they are in direct (yet covert) conflict with the health of the group.

Good night, Susan

P.S. You know what, I may just turn this into a blog post at some point.

LOOKING BRIGHT AND BREEZY THIS MORNING.

YOU TOO. SEE YOU LATER.

WHAT ARE YOU DOING HERE?

WELL, I'M DONE HERE --

-- LET'S GO TO MY OFFICE FOR A CHAT.

THIS IS YOUR OFFICE?

YEAH. GOOD PLACE TO GET AWAY FROM PRYING EYES AND EARS.

GETS PEOPLE OUT OF OFFICE MODE.

GOOD PLACE TO OBSERVE PEOPLE.

SURE YOU DON'T WANT ANY FOOD?

THEY DO GOOD SANDWICHES. CAKES TOO.

I'VE GOT STUFF BACK AT THE OFFICE.

I'LL EAT IT LATER.

FAIR ENOUGH.

SO, WAS THAT YOUR SISTER I SAW YOU WITH A WHILE BACK?

YOU LOOK ALIKE.

WE GET THAT A LOT.

WHY ARE WE HERE? WHY AM I BEING OBSERVED?

YOU DON'T LIKE BEING LOOKED AT?

EXCUSE ME?

SO TELL ME ABOUT YOUR APPROACH.

SOME OF IT DOESN'T MAKE SENSE.

I'M USING SOMETHING CALLED 'REAL OPTIONS'

HAVE YOU HEARD OF IT?

I'VE BEEN A PROJECT MANAGER FOR SOME TIME NOW --

-- I KNOW A VARIETY OF APPROACHES.

WHAT DO YOU MEAN BY 'REAL OPTIONS'?

SO, REAL OPTIONS IS THREE PRINCIPLES THAT FIT ON THE BACK OF A BUSINESS CARD.

THERE ARE A NUMBER OF PRACTICES THAT ARE THEN BASED ON THESE PRINCIPLES WHICH OUR PROJECT IS USING.

YES. YOU SEEM TO BE DOING A GOOD JOB OF IMPLEMENTING THEM.

WHAT SURPRISED ME THE MOST IS THAT REAL OPTIONS IS A RATIONAL DECISION PROCESS --

-- BUT IT TURNS OUT MOST PEOPLE ARE NOT RATIONAL.

AND I'M SURE MOST PEOPLE WOULD BE UPSET BY THAT.

153

Dear Susan,

Ever since Lilly explained real options to me my world view has been changing. I'm seeing options everywhere. It's like when you focus on the colour red all elements around you with that colour stand out more. You're adjusting your filter of perception. The same with options, when you know about them they seem to be everywhere. And what's worse is that I cannot unsee them anymore.

Everything seems to be optional when you start thinking about it. It just becomes a matter of what price are you willing to pay for a choice to be an option instead of a commitment. That price appears in many forms. If you treat a meeting with your friends as an option over and over again at some point they won't count on you as a friend being there. I need to be deliberate and open about what I do and why, otherwise people start seeing me as unreliable. When they know, they may just understand.

This abundance of available options is overwhelming. So much, that just last week I felt like I couldn't handle all the information. If everything is an option and I want to treat them as options I need to keep track of a lot of information. What I noticed myself doing, was not deciding at all. Almost like a decision paralysis, there is so much to choose from I can't decide and therefore I just don't.

And that was a very interesting realisation: I would rather not decide than choose something that wasn't the absolute best. That way I can't blame myself, but someone or something else. I would rather lose the benefit of choosing anything than taking responsibilty for the chance of making the "wrong" call. Is it that I'm afraid of the wrong call or am I just not comfortable with the uncertainty that I would rather choose avoiding the whole situation?

I came across a TED video on the web. Sheena Iyengar talked about some very interesting experiments she and her colleagues ran. They figured out that too much choice was a bad thing. Due to choice overload (or as I called it decision paralysis) people make worse choices even if making the choice is in their own best interest. Choice overload reduces engagement, decision quality and satisfaction. Also contrary to what I expected, more information doesn't help to make better choices. Visualisations however do help.

Turns out Barry Schwartz has similar ideas about decision making. He wrote the book "Paradox of Choice, why less is more". Read through it in one night. We are suffering from an overabundance of choice. While a little choice is better than having no choice, having too much choice puts the burden of choosing on the chooser. The chooser needs to invest time and energy into choosing only to expose the chooser to regret, escalation of expectations and self blame.

Both Barry Schwartz and Sheena Iyengar make similar recommendations. I have turned them into my own list:

* Be deliberate about what to treat as an option. Not everything that is optional needs to be treated as such.
* Be deliberate about making commitments. Making commitments nonreversible helps set my mind at ease.
* Don't expect too much.
* Allow myself to gradually get accustomed to options thinking.

While I like options thinking I need to learn how to pace my own learning in this.

Use option thinking for the important choices. Accept satisficing for many of the other choices. Just settle for an acceptable choice instead of trying to find the most optimal one.

Good night, Susan. Speak soon.

EXCEPT FOR THOSE PEOPLE WHO APPRECIATE UNCERTAINTY.

THANKFULLY THEY ARE ONLY FEW IN NUMBER.

REAL OPTIONS IS BASED ON FINANCIAL OPTION THEORY SUCH AS BLACK SCHOLES.

HOW DO YOU VALUE YOUR OPTIONS USING REAL OPTIONS?

I READ A GREAT COMIC STRIP ON THE DECISION-COACH BLOG ABOUT THIS.

ALTHOUGH WE KNOW OPTIONS HAVE A VALUE.

WE CANNOT USE FINANCIAL FORMULAS TO VALUE THEM.

ARE YOU ABLE TO EXPAND ON THAT?

WELL MANY REAL OPTIONS DO NOT HAVE AN UNDERLYING INSTRUMENT.

MOST HAVE AN EXPIRY CONDITION --

-- SUCH AS 'UNTIL CUBA HAS A REGIME CHANGE, OR THE BERLIN WALL COMES DOWN' --

-- RATHER THAN A CONTRACTUALLY SPECIFIED DATE AND TIME.

DOES THAT MEAN WE CANNOT COMPARE OPTIONS?

NOT AT ALL.

JUST DON'T GET HUNG UP DETERMINING THE FINANCIAL VALUE.

ACCEPT THAT IT'S NOT POSSIBLE TO GET AN ACCURATE FINANCIAL PRICE.

FOR EXAMPLE, WHAT IS MORE IMPORTANT TO YOU?

-- OR WINNING THAT BIG JOB?

DINNER WITH YOUR GIRLFRIEND ON VALENTINE'S NIGHT --

WELL, THAT'S AN EASY ONE --

I'M NOT IN A LONG TERM RELATIONSHIP AT THE MOMENT.

ANYWAY, YOU GET THE IDEA.

OH, EXCUSE ME...

THAT'S MY CUE, I'M AFRAID.

IS THAT IT?

EVERYTHING'S GREAT. GOT ALL I NEED.

ENJOY YOUR TEA.

I'LL SEE YOU AROUND.

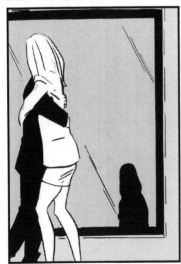

160

GOOD
LUNCH?

...FINE...

162

163

ROSE RANDALL'S BLOG

by any other name...

HOW TO VALUE REAL OPTIONS?

FOR THE PAST FEW DAYS I HAVE BEEN LOOKING INTO THE ORIGINS OF REAL OPTIONS, NAMELY FINANCIAL MATHEMATICS AND IN PARTICULAR THE BLACK-SCHOLES EQUATION. I FOUND NUMEROUS ARTICLES AND BLOGS WHERE THE AUTHORS EXPLAINED HOW TO PLUG THE NUMBERS INTO THE "BLACK-SCHOLES OPTION PRICE CALCULATOR" TO HELP PEOPLE VALUE THEIR REAL OPTIONS.

I STUMBLED ON A COMIC STRIP OF ALL THINGS ON THE BLOG OF WWW.DECISION-COACH.COM. THE TWO AUTHORS HAD WRITTEN A BLOG POST EXPLAINING WHY BLACK-SCHOLES IS WRONG FOR VALUING REAL OPTIONS.

FUNDAMENTALLY THE BLACK-SCHOLES EQUATION IS QUITE SIMPLE IN CONCEPT. SUPPOSE YOU CAN BUY AN OPTION. YOU HAVE THE RIGHT TO DO SOMETHING BUT NOT THE OBLIGATION. THE OPTION EXPIRES IN ONE YEAR FROM NOW. YOU HAVE ALREADY DETERMINED THAT THE DEAL HAS THREE POSSIBLE RESULTS: ONE RESULTING IN A RETURN OF NOTHING, ONE RESULTING IN $26 AND THE LAST POSSIBILITY IS A RETURN OF $100. NOW HOW MUCH IS HAVING THAT OPTION WORTH?

WHAT YOU NEED TO DO, IS WORK OUT THE RANGE OF POSSIBLE RESULTS AND ASSIGN THE PROBABILITY TO EACH RESULT OF THEM OCCURRING. LET'S PUT THESE IN THE TABLE BELOW. WE KNOW WE HAVE THREE POSSIBLE OUTCOMES: A, B, AND C. AND WE ALSO KNOW THE FINANCIAL RESULT OF EACH OF THESE. WITH SOME RESEARCH WE CAN FIGURE OUT THE PROBABILITIES OF EACH OF THE OUTCOMES. MULTIPLY THE VALUE OF EACH RESULT BY THE PROBABILITY OF IT OCCURRING AND ADD THEM UP. THE RESULT OF THAT SUM IS THE FUTURE VALUE, IN THIS CASE $33.

ARCHIVES

MARCH (1)

FEBRUARY (1)

JANUARY (2)

Option Outcome	Result	Result Probability	Value
A	$0	0.3	$0
B	$26	0.5	$13
C	$100	0.2	$20
Sum	N/A	N/A	$33

PREVIOUS YEAR (7)

WE'RE NOT DONE JUST YET. THE OPTION IS WORTH $33 IN THE FUTURE ONE
YEAR FROM NOW. HOW MUCH IS IT WORTH NOW?
FOR THIS CALCULATION LET'S ASSUME THE INTEREST RATE IS 10%, MEANING
FOR $100 YOU PUT IN YOUR BANK ACCOUNT YOU'LL RECEIVE $10 IN INTEREST,
SO YOU THEN HAVE $110.

HOW MUCH MONEY WOULD YOU NEED TO PUT IN YOUR BANK ACCOUNT TODAY
TO GET $33 IN A YEAR IF THE INTEREST RATE IS 10%?

IT'S $30. SO HAVING THE OPTION TODAY IS WORTH $30.

THIS DOESN'T SOUND COMPLICATED. CAN YOU BELIEVE THE GUYS WHO CAME
UP WITH THE BLACK-SCHOLES FORMULA RECEIVED A NOBEL PRIZE FOR IT?
WHERE'S THE CATCH? THE ANSWER IS IN CALCULATING THE PROBABILITIES
THAT ARE USED. WHILE IN THE EXAMPLE WE SAID YOU CAME UP WITH THE
PROBABILITIES, CALCULATION OF THE PROBABILITIES IS A LOT HARDER THAN IT
SOUNDS AND INVOLVES SOME FAIRLY ADVANCED CONCEPTS LIKE MARKOV
CHAINS, ITO'S LEMMA, GIRSARNOV'S THEORY AND THE CONCEPT OF RISK
NEUTRALITY. RISK NEUTRALITY MEANS USING THE PROBABILITIES THAT BOOK-
IES USE IN HORSE RACING RATHER THAN TRYING TO FIND THE REAL PROBABILI-
TIES. FINDING THE REAL PROBABILITIES IS IMPOSSIBLE WITHOUT A TIME
MACHINE.

IN THEIR COMIC STRIP, THE REAL OPTIONS AUTHORS POINT OUT THAT
BLACK-SCHOLES WORKS WELL IN FINANCIAL MARKETS FOR SOME TECHNICAL
REASONS. IN THE REAL WORLD LIQUIDITY COMPLETELY DOMINATES THE
EQUATION. IN FACT ALL OF THE ASSUMPTIONS IN THE BLACK-SCHOLES AND
ALL OF THE INPUTS TO THE EQUATION ARE INVALID WHEN YOU MOVE OUT OF
THE FINANCIAL WORLD AND INTO THE REAL WORLD OF REAL OPTIONS. IN AN
AMUSING VIDEO, THE AUTHORS MAKE THE POINT BY DEMONSTRATING THAT
THERE IS PRETTY MUCH NO WAY OF VALUING A BOTTLE OF WATER. A BOTTLE
OF WATER COULD BE WORTHLESS OR WORTH A PERSON'S LIFE DEPENDING ON
CONTEXT. AS A THOUGHT, HOW DO YOU VALUE THE OPTION TO KISS
SOMEONE?

THE AUTHORS ALSO MAKE THE POINT THAT BLACK-SCHOLES IS DANGEROUS
BECAUSE ITS COMPLEXITY CAN DETER PEOPLE FROM CHALLENGING
VALUATIONS.

ARCHIVES

MARCH (1)

FEBRUARY (1)

JANUARY (2)

PREVIOUS YEAR
(7)

171

CHAPTER SEVEN

174

EXCUSE ME?

THAT'S NOT VERY ROMANTIC -- -- I THINK YOU NEED A BETTER LINE.

LILLY!!

YOU SAID EVERYTHING WAS OKAY! WHAT CHANGED?!

WHAT DID YOU TELL THEM??!

NOTHING! I DIDN'T GET THE CHANCE.

THEY JUST SAID THAT THE BIGGEST CLIENT HAS CHANGED HER MIND AND IS STOPPING THEIR FUNDING.

THEY GIVE A REASON?

SAID IT WAS TOO RISKY.

WHY WOULD THEY SAY THAT?

I DON'T KNOW. BUT THAT'S ALL WHAT THEY SAID.

THANK YOU.

I MAY BE A LITTLE DRUNK, BUT I BELIEVE HIM.

WHY DIDN'T YOU TELL ME BACK AT THE OFFICE?

I TRIED TO, BUT YOU'D LEFT.

I TRIED CALLING, BUT YOU DIDN'T ANSWER.

AFTER I GOT YOUR ADDRESS FROM SOMEONE ON YOUR TEAM, I CAME HERE.

WHEN DID YOU CALL?

I'VE HAD MY PHONE WITH ME ALL DAY.

...AH...

IT'S ON SILENT...

176

TYPICAL.

HAVE YOU BEEN HERE ALL NIGHT?

PRETTY MUCH.

I NEEDED TO MAKE SURE ROSE WASN'T WALKING INTO A FIRING SQUAD.

DIDN'T WANT TO BE BLAMED.

REALLY...

AHHHH... WHILE THIS IS VERY TOUCHING, ANY CHANCE WE CAN GO INSIDE?

REALLY NEED THE TOILET.

FINE.

SO, YOU MUST BE ROSE'S SISTER.

...MUST BE...

178

RIGHT, THAT SEEMS TO BE EVERYONE.

MORNING ALL.

NEED TO HAVE A MEETING BEFORE WE GET STARTED.

BIT OF BAD NEWS TO START THE DAY.

THE BOARD IS MEETING THE BIGGEST FUNDER OF OUR PROJECT IN A WEEK'S TIME TO FORMALISE THE TERMINATION OF THEIR FUNDING.

YOU MEAN WE HAVE TO START AGAIN ON SOMETHING NEW...?

NO. SHE MEANS THAT WE ALL HAVE TO FIND A NEW JOB.

NOW, NOW.

AS I SAID WE'RE STILL A WEEK AWAY FROM ANYTHING FORMAL.

SO AS FAR AS EVERYONE ELSE IS CONCERNED, IT'S STILL BUSINESS AS USUAL.

BUT AS WE'VE BEEN GIVEN A BIT OF A HEADS UP, WE HAVE UNTIL THEN TO FIND AN OPTION.

THAT DOESN'T SEEM LIKELY --

-- I HAVE A MORTGAGE TO PAY AND A BABY ON THE WAY.

180

YOU GET REDEPLOYED TO OTHER PROJECTS --

-- SO YOU MIGHT WANT TO SALVAGE SOME OF THE WORK YOU'VE DONE FOR SOMEWHERE ELSE.

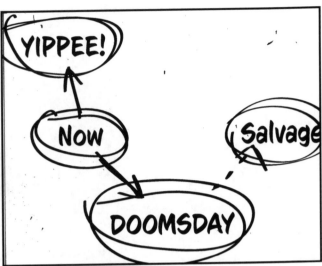

YIPPEE!

NOW

Salvage

DOOMSDAY

YEAH, BUT I WOULD RATHER HAVE REDUNDANCY --

--THAN HAVE TO WORK FOR THE IDIOT ON THE FOURTH FLOOR.

I THINK WE CAN WORK WITH THESE.

LET'S START TO PREPARE FOR EACH OF THESE SCENARIOS --

-- AND IF WE THINK OF ANYTHING ELSE WE CAN WORK ON THEM AS WELL.

YIPPEE!

NOW

Salvage

DOOMSDAY

Redundancy

Work with idiots...

FOR THE SACKING SCENARIO LET'S ALL GET OUR RESUMES UP TO SCRATCH.

REVIEW THEM WITH COLLEAGUES AND SHARE CONTACTS FOR FINDING ANOTHER JOB.

EACH OF YOU BUILD MOMENTUM TO FIND A JOB RATHER THAN FIND YOURSELF UNEMPLOYED WITH NO DIRECTION ON DAY ONE THAT WILL LOSE YOU VALUABLE TIME.

FOR THOSE WHO ARE CONSIDERING TAKING THE REDUNDANCY, YOU MAY WANT TO FIND OUT WHAT THE JOB MARKET IS LIKE BEFORE YOU MAKE THE DECISION TO TAKE REDUNDANCY RATHER THAN THE OTHER JOB OFFER.

FOR THE SALVAGE STRATEGY, I WILL START TO PACKAGE UP THE WORK WE COULD USE ON OTHER PROJECTS.

I'LL ALSO CHECK WITH THE LEGAL TEAM TO SEE WHAT IS ALLOWED AND WHAT IS NOT ALLOWED.

IF IT GOES BAD, OUR WORK MIGHT BE PUT BEYOND LEGAL REACH WHEN BOTH PARTIES START ARGUING ABOUT WHO'S THE OWNER OF THE WORK AND NOBODY IS ALLOWED TO TOUCH IT.

A BIT OF WORK NOW MIGHT MEAN WE CAN STILL USE IT AFTER THE PROJECT GETS CANCELLED.

YEAH, BUT I'D RATHER THEY DID NOT CANCEL THE PROJECT.

WE ALL AGREE BUT IF REALITY ISN'T AS WE'D LIKE IT --

-- WE SHOULD PREPARE FOR EACH SCENARIO WE IDENTIFY.

SPLIT INTO GROUPS OF TWO OR THREE AND THEN WE'LL GET BACK TOGETHER IN AN HOUR.

I KNOW IT'S NOT GLAMOUROUS, BUT CAN YOU PLEASE HEAD OUT FOR SOME SUPPLIES?

I HAVEN'T GOT ENOUGH CASH FOR THE WHOLE CLASS.

JUST GRAB MY PURSE FROM MY BAG. SHOULD BE ENOUGH IN THERE.

I'LL FIND OUT WHAT PEOPLE WANT THEN GIVE YOU A HAND. MIGHT AS WELL MAKE MYSELF USEFUL.

YOU WANT A TEA?

THANKS.

NO PROBLEM. SEE YOU IN A BIT.

185

Blobs

RANDOM MUSINGS - LILLY RANDALL

Increasing your psychic odds with Scenario Planning

Do you consider yourself a psychic? Having the ability to predict the future means you don't have to guess what happens next. You can make predictions knowing that your imagination and reality always match up.

Most of us have had experiences where a situation we thought about carefully turned out to be completely different in reality than we had imagined. It happens multiple times a day. We have that experience over and over.

While we think, plan and imagine a lot, reality almost never aligns with our imagination. Sadly when this happens we are not prepared. Our pursuit of a perfect world leaves us unprepared for the world we did not want. How to avoid this painful situation... Scenario Planning.

Scenario Planning

Scenario Planning is an another expression of real options. Like many set based design and other commitment deferment processes, it pre-dates real options by many, many years.

Scenario Planning was first popularised by Peter Senge's book "The Fifth Discipline". In the book, Peter describes how Royal Dutch Shell (spearheaded by Arie De Geus, head of the Strategic Planning Group) creates a number of scenarios which are then taught to the entire organisation. The whole organisation can then think about how they would respond to these scenarios.

All of these scenarios could become true. Having these scenarios allows Shell to prepare for worlds they like, and for worlds they will not like. As part of their preparation they may need to build options.

Preparing for the possible

The scenarios are massive, earth moving events that could shake Shell to its core, and destroy it if they are not prepared. Scenarios like "A Third World War breaks out" or "Oil hits $1000 a barrel" or "Oil runs out" have a tremendous effect on a large oil corporation.

These scenarios had the interesting effect that the organisation started communicating and collaborating in ways that it had not seen before. The creation of risk management scenarios has immediate positive benefits beyond just being better prepared for a possible future.

Scaling Scenario Thinking

This kind of Scenario Analysis (or risk management) can be applied at any scale. From the individual, up to the corporation, and finally to the global scale. From "I want to be a footballer" to "The Currents in the Atlantic turn off and cause an Ice Age".

Wouldn't it be great if every school child in the world were to imagine a world where an Ice Age occurred. If everyone talked about a single thing. Imagine the collaboration it would bring.

Increasing your odds in the future

Talking and reading about it makes sense. Let's be honest how often do you only prepare for a single future? Inspect plans and budgets of any company: how many futures are they prepared for?

Don't bet on a single future. Prepare for multiple possible futures and have your options for each in place. You have just increased your chances of predicting the future!

Seeya next time -

L

NOW WE HAVE OUR PERSONAL SCENARIOS IN PLACE, LET'S FOCUS ON FIXING THE PROBLEM FOR THE PROJECT AND SEE WHAT WE CAN DO IN THE TIME LEFT.

THIS IS A TERRIBLE SITUATION BUT I THINK IT WOULD BE WORSE WITHOUT THE OPTIONS WE ARE CREATING.

WITHOUT THEM, THE UNCERTAINTY WOULD BE KILLING ME.

I EVEN CONSIDERED GOING TO SEE A PALM READER.

YEP. WHEN IT LAST HAPPENED TO ME THE WHOLE PROJECT FROZE.

WE ARE STARTING TO THINK MORE ABOUT OPTIONS AND PUSHING COMMITMENTS OUT AS FAR AS IT IS SENSIBLE TO, AND GATHERING INFORMATION WHILE WE DO THAT.

IT FEELS LIKE WE ARE IN UNCHARTED TERRITORY WHERE WE ARE USING THE PRINCIPLES RATHER THAN THE PRACTICES.

YES. AND I THINK WE ARE STARTING TO INTERNALISE THEM AS WELL.

EVERYTHING I LOOK AT NOW I THINK OF AS EITHER AN OPTION OR A COMMITMENT.

AND FOR EVERY COMMITMENT, WE LOOK FOR OPTIONS TO MAKE IT REVERSIBLE.

PRETTY COOL, SIS --

-- SPOKEN LIKE A TRUE MASTER.

YOU HAVE TWO COMPETITORS WHO ARE UPDATING THEIR PRODUCT EVERY MONTH WHILST YOU HAVE NOT UPDATED YOURS FOR A YEAR.

WE THOUGHT YOU WERE UPDATING YOUR SOFTWARE WITH OUR WEEKLY RELEASES, BUT YOU DIDN'T.

OUR UNDERSTANDING IS THAT IF THIS CONTINUES FOR ANOTHER YEAR, YOU WILL LOSE ALL OF YOUR MARKET SHARE.

EXACTLY, WHICH IS WHY WE CANNOT RISK LOSING IT BEFORE THEN.

WE HOPE TO HOLD ON AS LONG AS POSSIBLE.

WHICH IS WHY WE NEED TO IMPLEMENT THE SOLUTION WE ARE BUILDING WHICH WILL ALLOW YOU TO JUMP AHEAD OF YOUR COMPETITORS AND THEN RELEASE ON A WEEKLY BASIS TO KEEP AHEAD.

YES. BUT WE CANNOT LOSE THE LAST BIT OF THE MARKET.

OUR APPROACH TO RISK MANAGEMENT IS TO CONSIDER THE POSSIBLE SCENARIOS, AND BUILD AN OPTION FOR EACH.

HOW DOES THIS WORK?

CLKK

192

194

SO, HEARD THE GOOD NEWS.

WELL....

WE GOT A COUPLE OF DAYS.

BETTER THAN NOTHING.

MEANS YOU CAN RELAX FOR A COUPLE OF DAYS.

WHOPPEE....

I MUST REMEMBER TO HAVE SOME FUN.

GIVE YOU AN OPPORTUNITY TO GO TO THE CINEMA.

SHAME TO WASTE IT AS IT'S ON YOUR DOORSTEP.

UH... I'M USUALLY NO GOOD AT THIS SORT OF THING --

-- BUT ARE YOU TRYING TO ASK ME OUT?

NO, NO. NOTHING LIKE THAT...

IF I WAS GOING TO ASK YOU OUT, I'D SUGGEST DINNER.

...OKAY THEN...

THERE ARE A FEW PLACES TO EAT NEAR YOUR FLAT.

ANY RECOMMENDATIONS?

196

197

DOOLLIUP DOOLLIUP
DOOLLIUP DOOLLIUP

ROSE
RANDALL.

201

OKAY. OKAY.

THANK YOU.

TKK

WE HAVE A GO DATE!

THE PROJECT HAS JUST BEEN UN-CANCELLED!!

DO WE CELEBRATE NOW?

WE CELEBRATE WHEN WE'RE DONE.

SPOILSPORT!

I'LL GO OUT TO GRAB SOME COFFEES. MAYBE A CAKE OR TEN. WE CAN RELAX --

-- BUT IT'S NOT A CELEBRATION YET.

FAIR ENOUGH...

FIND OUT WHAT PEOPLE WANT, I'LL GO AND SPREAD THE GOOD NEWS...

202

THANK YOU FOR COMING TO THE PROJECT RETROSPECTIVE.

EVEN THOUGH WE'VE DONE ONE EVERY RELEASE THIS ONE IS FOR THE WHOLE PROJECT.

WE WILL LOOK AT THINGS THAT WENT WELL THAT WE WANT TO CONTINUE DOING --

-- SO THAT THE COMPANY CAN IMPROVE FUTURE PROJECTS.

OKAY.

NOW WE ARE FINISHED, CAN WE CELEBRATE?

OKAY. IT'S TLC TIME.

CAN I HAVE YOUR ATTENTION PLEASE --

-- I'M SORRY TO INTERRUPT YOUR PARTY BUT WE HAVE AN ANNOUNCEMENT.

WHAT IS IT?

I AM SORRY TO SAY THAT AT THE REQUEST OF THE CLIENT, ROSE HAS BEEN SACKED FROM THE PROJECT.

WHAT?

I'M SORRY, BUT IT WAS THE ONLY WAY WE COULD PROMOTE YOU SO THAT YOU COULD LEAD OUR NEXT PROGRAMME OF WORK.

I DON'T UNDERSTAND...

EVERYBODY, PLEASE RAISE YOUR GLASSES FOR ROSE --

-- OUR NEWEST VICE PRESIDENT!

PRETTY GOOD, SIS. TOLD YOU YOU'D COME UP TRUMPS.

THAT YOU DID.

YOU KEEP ON WITH THIS, SEE WHERE IT TAKES YOU.

DON'T MEAN BE THE BLACK CLOUD, BUT IT DOESN'T ALWAYS TURN OUT FOR THE BEST.

WILL YOU SHUT UP?! YOU KNOW HOW LONG IT'S TAKEN ME TO GET HER TO THIS?!!

SORRY, BUT WHAT I'M TRYING TO SAY IS THAT AS ROSE TOOK A DOOMED PROJECT AND COMPLETELY TURNED IT AROUND. THERE'S A CHANCE THAT SHE'D GET LUMBERED DEALING WITH ALL THE LOST CAUSES --

-- IT CAN BECOME A BIT OVERWHELMING.

SOUNDS LIKE YOU'RE SPEAKING FROM PERSONAL EXPERIENCE.

HOW YOU THINK I GOT HERE IN THE FIRST PLACE?!

YOU'RE SAYING I WAS A LOST CAUSE...?

WELL YOU'RE WEREN'T COMPLETELY WITHOUT HOPE..

OH... HE'S A KEEPER...

EPILOGUE

YOU SHOULD GET SOMETHING GREEN. IT'LL SHOW OFF YOUR TAN BETTER.

I'M NOT GOING OUT THERE TO SUN BATHE.

DON'T WORRY, IT'LL COME NATURAL.

YOU'LL BE TURNING HEADS IN NO TIME.

NEW LINES ADDED

YOU SAYING I DON'T ALREADY?

OOOHHH LOOK AT YOU! ONE BRUSH WITH SUCCESS AND YOU'VE TURNED INTO A RIGHT LITTLE DIVA!!

HA...

WELL IT'S GOOD TO SEE YOU MORE CONFIDENT. MAKES YOU MORE OPEN.

I CAN SEE. IT'S PRETTY GOOD HOW MUCH YOU'VE CHANGED IN JUST A FEW MONTHS.

.. I TRY...

I KNOW SOME BODY THAT WOULD BE GLAD TO HEAR ABOUT YOUR EXPERIENCE.

REALLY? WHO?

HOW MUCH TLC CAN YOU HANDLE?!

The Learning Cantina

EUROPEAN -EXPO

09-11th Ma

210

211

WELL, WHERE DO I BEGIN...?

THE END

(FOR NOW)

Afterword

Wow! What a trip this has been. What started as a brief look at the library of a friend in August 2004 resulted in what you have just read almost nine years later. If you want to know what the chain of events is, ask us when you meet us.

You have made it to the end of the book. We hope you enjoyed it as much as we have creating it. If you have any questions or comments, we love to hear them, So please send them to info@commitment-thebook.com

For extra material please visit our support website at http://commitment-thebook.com/support

Each version of the book has a version number in the front of the book. Any changes or updates made in the future are listed at: http://commitment-thebook.com/updates

About the Authors

Olav Maassen is General Manager, EMEA at VersionOne in the Netherlands and he has more than ten years of experience consulting mainly for financial institutions.

You can follow Olav on twitter at @OlavMaassen

Chris Matts is a consultant who specializes in developing risk management and trading systems for investment banks.

You can follow Chris on twitter at @PapaChrisMatts

Chris Geary is a London-based, experienced graphic artist. He attended the London Cartoon Centre, mainly under the tutorage of David Lloyd.

You can follow Chris on twitter at @ChrisAGeary

Acknowledgements

This is where we get to thank all the people who have supported us and / or have suffered from us creating this book.

First we like to thank all our patrons supporting us through crowdfunding part of the creation of the book: Pollyanna Pixton, Sue McKinney, Jurgen Maassen, Leny Verhage, Yves Hanoulle, Torbjorn Gyllebring, Ola Ellnestam, Gabrielle Benefield, César Idrovo Carrillo, Hakan Forss, Laurens Bonnema, Graham Oakes, Kent McDonald, Simon Kirk, Robert Holler, Pieter Rijken, Steven List, Julie Chickering, Christopher Avery, Jenni Jepsen, Norbert Winklareth, Niel Nickolaisen, Ketil Jensen, John McFadyen, Nils Christian Haugen, Kingsley Hendrickse, Andreas Larsson, John Connolly, Nicholas Coutts, Nick Scott, Christian Blunden, J.B. Rainsberger, Nick de Voil, Darren Hobbs, Jeffrey Anderson, Todd Little, Yann Picard de Muller, Aki Salmi, Andrew Turner, Jasper Sonnevelt, Kristian Haugaard, Liz Keogh, and Jon Terry. You all have given us the push at the start that we needed.

Second we are hugely grateful for the effort our translators have put into their work. While we were writing the book, these people have simultaneously read all the words and translated them: Erwin van der Koogh, Jan De Baere, Jade de Baere, Olaf Lewitz, Michael Leber, Mads Troels Hansen, Hans Haller Baggesen, Kjell Lauren, Henrik Taubert, Tonje Skoenberg, Johannes Brodwall, Toni Tassani, Alejandro Scandroli, Fermin Saez, Claudio Perrone, Antonio Lucca, Franck Depierre, Pierre Fauvel, Catia Oliveira, Oana Juncu, Flavius Stef, Ivana Gancheva, Dimitar Bakardzhiev, Marcin Sanecki, Marcin Floryan, Zsolt Fabok, Gaspar Nagy, Alexei Zheglov, Sergey Kotlov, and Elad Sofer.

Also we would like to thank the following people for providing very valuable and sometimes harsh feedback that made this book so much better: all of the translators (again), Linda van de Burgwal, Mary Gorman, Jarl Meijer, Geert Bossuyt, Luke Hohmann, César Idrovo Carrillo (again), Jurgen Maassen (again), Will Britton, Douglas Squirrel, and all others who have submitted feedback.

Olav Maassen:
Thank you Ingrid, Niels and Britt for understanding and supporting this project and Ingrid for being a partner in this journey called life.

Chris Matts:
To Mr P for all the love and support.
And my Mum and Dad of course who still don't know what I do for a living.

Chris Geary:
Special thanks for everyone's support over the years.

Bibliography

Anderson, D.J. (2010). Kanban. Sequim: Blue Hole Press
Barlow, S., Parry, S. & Faulkner, M. (2005). Sense and Respond. New York: Palgrave Macmillan
Brooks, F. P. (1975). The Mythical Man-Month. Boston: Addison Wesley Longman
Chambris, C. & Simons D. (2010). The Invisible Gorilla. London: HarperCollins Publishers
Constantine, L.L. (2001). The Peopleware Papers. Upper Saddle River: Yourdon Press
Covey, S.R. (1989). The Seven Habits of Highly Effective People. New York: Fireside
DeMarco, T. (2002). Slack. New York: Broadway
DeMarco, T. & Lister, T. (2003). Waltzing with Bears. New York: Dorset House Publishing
Federman, M. & De Kerckhove, D. (2003). McLuhan for Managers. Toronto: Viking Canada
Fields, J. (2011). Uncertainty. New York: Penguin Group
Gerstein, M. & Ellsberg, M. (2008). Flirting with Disaster. New York: Union Square Press
Gilbert, D. (2005). Stumbling on Happiness. New York: Vintage Books
Gladwell, M. (2005). Blink. New York: Little, Brown and Company
Goldratt, e., Cox, J. (1986). The Goal. New York: North River Press
Hammond, J.S., Keeney, R.L. & Raiffa, H. (1999). Smart Choices. Boston: Harvard Business School Press
Harford, T. (2011). Adapt. London: Little, Brown
Heath, D. & Heath, C. (2007). Made to Stick. Why Some Ideas Survive and Others Die. New York: Random House
Hull, J. (1997). Options, Futures and Other Derivatives. Upper Saddle River: Pearson Education
Iyengar, S. (2010). The Art of Choosing. London: Little, Brown and Company
MacKenzie, G. (1996). Orbiting the Giant Hairball. New York: Penguin Group
Mlodinow, L. (2008). The Drunkard's Walk, How Randomness Rules Our Lives. New York: Vintage Books
Pixton, P., Nickolaisen, N., Little, T. & McDonald, K. (2009). Stand Back and Deliver. Boston: Addison Wesley
Plous, S. (1993). The Psychology of Judgment and Decision Making. New York: McGraw-Hill
Reinertsen, D. (1997). Managing the Design Factory. New York: The Free Press
Schelling, T.C. (1960). Strategy of Conflict. Cambridge: Harvard University
Schwartz, B. (2004). The Paradox of Choice: Why More is Less. New York: HarperCollins Publishers
Schwartz, B. & Sharpe, K. (2010). Practical Wisdom: The Right Way to Do the Right Thing. New York: Riverhead Books
Senge, P. (1990). The Fifth Discipline. Milsons Point: Random House Australia
Smith, P.G. & Reinertsen, D.G. (1998). Developing Products in Half the Time, 2nd ed. New York: John Wiley & Sons, Inc.
Taleb, N.N. (2007). Black Swan. New York: Random House
Taleb, N.N. (2004). Fooled by Randomness. New York: Random House
Thaler, R.H. & Sunstein, C.R. (2008). Nudge. London: Penguin Group
Yourdon, E. (1997). Death March. New Jersey: Prentice Hall Inc.
Watanabe, K (2009). Problem Solving 101: A Simple book for Smart People. New York: Penguin Group
Zimbardo, Ph. & Boyd, J. (2008). The Time Paradox. New York: Free Press

Bibliography about form

Abel, J. & Madden, M. (2008). Drawing words & Writing Pictures. New York: First Second

Kawasaki, G. & Welch, S. (2013). APE: Author, Publisher, Entrepeneur - How to Publish a Book. Nononina Press

McCloud, S. (1993). Making Comics: Storytelling Secrets of Comics, Manga and Graphic Novels. New York: William Morrow Paperbacks

McCloud, S. (2000). Reinventing Comics: How Imagination and Technology are Revolutionizing an Art Form. New York: William Morrow Paperbacks

McCloud, S. (1993). Understanding Comics: the Invisible Art. New York: HarperPerennial

McKee, R. (1997). Story. New York: HarperCollins

Vogler, C. (1998). The Writer's Journey: Mythic Structure for Writers. Studio City: Michael Wiese Productions

Made in the USA
Charleston, SC
21 September 2016